Praise for *A Dream of Undying Fame*

"A thoughtful and incisive assessment of psychoanalytic theory and practice, its permanent contributions, and its serious flaws. In highly accessible language and style, Louis Breger leads us through Freud's early experiences, which were to influence his later theories, and his dreams of martial glory, giving due credit to Joseph Breuer, the first practitioner of the talking cure. He sets us straight on the often distorted history of Anna O. and Freud's infatuation with his male friends while appraising the validity of his theories as they developed along the way. Readers who appreciate a serious scientific book that reads like a detective thriller will be totally captured by *A Dream of Undying Fame*."

—Sophie Freud, Professor Emerita at the
Simmons College School of Social Work,
author of *Living in the Shadow of the Freud Family*

"Louis Breger's compassionate, brilliant and spellbinding retelling of the origins of psychoanalysis, seen through the lens of Freud's trauma history, intense longings, and profound ambition, should be required reading for anyone interested in the foundations of one of the most influential theories of the 20th century. By telling the story of Freud and his relationships, Breger both challenges the dogmas that have stymied so many psychoanalytic historians, and illuminates the dynamics and entanglements at the heart of psychoanalysis' marvelous breadth and inherent limitations."

—Arietta Slade, Professor of Clinical Psychology,
City University of New York

A DREAM OF
UNDYING FAME

ALSO BY LOUIS BREGER

Clinical Cognitive Psychology
(editor)

The Effect of Stress on Dreams
(with I. Hunter and R. W. Lane)

From Instinct to Identity:
The Development of Personality

Freud's Unfinished Journey: Conventional and
Critical Perspectives in Psychoanalytic Theory

Dostoevsky: The Author as Psychoanalyst

Freud: Darkness in the Midst of Vision

A Dream of Undying Fame

How Freud Betrayed His Mentor and Invented Psychoanalysis

LOUIS BREGER

BASIC BOOKS

A Member of the Perseus Books Group
New York

Published by
Basic Books, A Member of the Perseus Books Group
387 Park Avenue South
New York, NY 10016

Books published by Basic Books are available at special discounts for
bulk purchases in the United States by corporations, institutions, and
other organizations. For more information, please contact the Special
Markets Department at the Perseus Books Group, 2300 Chestnut Street,
Suite 200, Philadelphia, PA 19103, or call (800) 255-1514, or e-mail
special.markets@perseusbooks.com.

Designed by Timm Bryson

Library of Congress Cataloging-in-Publication Data
Breger, Louis, 1931-
    A dream of undying fame : how Freud betrayed his mentor and invented
psychoanalysis / Louis Breger.
        p. ; cm.
    Includes bibliographical references and index.
    ISBN-13: 978-0-465-01735-5 (alk. paper)
    ISBN-10: 0-465-01735-5 (alk. paper)
    1. Freud, Sigmund, 1856-1939. 2. Breuer, Josef, 1842-1925. 3. Freud, Sigmund, 1856-
1939. Studien über Hysteria. 4. Psychoanalysts—Biography. 5. Psychoanalysis—History.
I. Title.
    [DNLM: 1. Freud, Sigmund, 1856-1939. 2. Breuer, Josef, 1842-1925. 3. Freud,
Sigmund, 1856-1939. Studien über Hysteria. 4. Psychoanalysis—Biography.
5. Psychoanalysis—history. 6. History, 19th Century. 7. History, 20th Century.
WZ 100 B8335d 2009]
    BF109.F74.B737 2009
    150.19'52092—dc22
    [B]

                                        2009019970

10 9 8 7 6 5 4 3 2 1

If his inmost heart could have been laid open, there would have been discovered that dream of undying fame; which dream as it is, is more powerful than a thousand realities.

NATHANIEL HAWTHORNE
Fanshawe, 1828

The expectation of eternal fame was so beautiful, as was that of certain wealth, complete independence, and lifting the children above the severe worries that robbed me of my youth. Everything depended upon whether or not hysteria would come out right.

SIGMUND FREUD
letter to Wilhelm Fliess, 1897

FOR BARBARA

Muse, Collaborator, and True Love

CONTENTS

CHAPTER ONE

Exploring the Irrational

For one who lived among enemies so long;
If often he was wrong and at times absurd,
To us he is no more a person
Now but a whole climate of opinion.
                    W. H. AUDEN
            In Memory of Sigmund Freud, 1940

Sigmund Freud's ideas had a revolutionary impact on twentieth-century thought and culture. He demonstrated the many manifestations of the unconscious; created a method of psychoanalytic treatment; and developed a wide-ranging theory that revealed the meaning found in symptoms, sexual life, dreams, fantasies, childhood, art, and literature. Like Johannes Kepler in astronomy and Charles Darwin in biology, he radically altered our understanding of our place in the world, overturning the view of humans as rational, conscious beings.

Yet few people today are aware that many of the essential features of psychoanalysis were first invented by Freud's older colleague, Josef Breuer, and can be found in the groundbreaking book they coauthored in 1895, *Studies on Hysteria*. In the lectures he gave on his trip to America in 1909, Freud said:

> If it is a merit to have brought psycho-analysis into being, that merit
> is not mine. I had no share in its earliest beginnings. I was a student

and working for my final examinations at the time when another Viennese physician, Dr. Josef Breuer, first—in 1880–[188]2—made use of this procedure on a girl who was suffering from hysteria.

This is the plain truth, yet in subsequent publications, when his drive for fame had become more powerful, Freud gave a sinister twist to Breuer's work with this patient and increasingly took credit as the sole inventor of psychoanalysis. He rejected Breuer's ideas and approach to treatment, setting the field on an unfortunate course that was only corrected many years later.

Freud's concepts continue to have a hold on the popular imagination. Psychological treatment is frequently referred to as being "on the couch," and numerous cartoons about psychotherapy show a patient—who may be human, dog, or cat—lying down, with a bearded man sitting behind the couch, taking notes. This image persists even though classical psychoanalysis, with its couch and Freud look-alike, has been dwindling to the point of oblivion over the last few decades. Psychotherapy is increasingly conducted face to face and is not Freudian in the traditional sense. The silent, severe psychoanalyst, who presumably knows the deepest secrets of one's unconscious, is no longer a revered icon. Those aspects of the theory that are most captivating intellectually—Eros and Thanatos or the life and death instincts, libidinal energy, phallic and vaginal symbols, the primal scene, penis envy, latent homosexuality—are more alive now in departments of literature than in the consulting rooms of therapists.

At the same time, many of Freud's other concepts—unconscious motives; the id, ego, and superego; oral and anal stages of development; the Oedipus complex; defense and repression; the Freudian slip; the couch and the fifty-minute hour—have passed into popular culture and are often used without an awareness of their origins or implications. A man can't find his car keys when planning to visit his mother, so a friend says, "Aha, you really hate her," to which he replies, "Don't get all Freudian on me." A young woman I was seeing in therapy described her boyfriend as "anal," meaning he was always punctual. She had no idea that the term comes from an essay by Freud in which compulsive neatness, orderliness, and cleanliness are traced to the "anal stage" of psychosexual development, a provocative but mainly unsupported idea. The technical rules of analysis have also permeated the popular domain: the therapist's relative silence and detachment; a strict schedule of fees; the fixed hour (now down to forty-five minutes); explanations focused entirely on early childhood, to the neglect of current life experiences such as discrimination, poverty, or the traumas of war; and interpretations of a wide range of diseases as "emotional," "psychological," or "all in your head." Psychoanalysis has always been a mixed bag: valuable insights coexisting with overblown theories; ideas that liberated people from old sexual taboos alongside harmful stereotypes about women. As Auden put it, "he was often wrong and at times absurd," but became "a whole climate of opinion."

Theories about human behavior and disturbance are influenced by the personality of the theorist in a way that those in many other fields are not. The truth of the theories of gravity and natural selection is independent of the kind of men Isaac Newton and Charles Darwin were. Jonas Salk's vaccine for polio is effective regardless of what he was like as a person. Psychology is not like that. Our ideas about personality and psychotherapy are intertwined with our own cultural values and life experiences; we can move beyond inclinations, preconceptions, and emotional reactions— gain some degree of distance and objectivity—but our personal histories exert their influence, all the more so when they are unconscious. We need to keep our minds open to alternative theories and be aware of other factors that influence our approaches.

Some years ago a group of colleagues and I were chatting about ourselves when it came out that all six of us had depressed mothers. We concluded that our choice to save, cure, or help people in psychological distress was shaped by this central childhood experience. Others who choose the career of psychotherapist have suffered serious illnesses; had sick or disturbed parents or siblings; had alcoholic fathers; were abandoned or neglected; found themselves caught in the middle of parental warfare; or were physically, emotionally, or sexually abused. The list of influences is long and varied, yet each person's background determined this career choice, as well as the particular kind of theory and practice he or she follows.

Freud is no exception in this regard. His personal history, as well as his social background, influenced both the theories he developed and the kind of treatment he practiced. For example, several of the patients described in *Studies on Hysteria* suffered the death of loved ones or other severe losses that reverberated emotionally with his own life. With these women he both approached and retreated from the emotional traumas that resonated with his own childhood. He constructed psychoanalysis from a combination of observation of patients and his understanding—and misunderstanding—of himself. His famous self-analysis, carried out just after the publication of *Studies*, is a clear example of this. Freud discovered many important things about himself during the self-analysis, while simultaneously pulling back from others—such as the losses he suffered as a child—that were too frightening. What he could see and not see, what he could know and not know, were the basis for the duality and contradictions that run through his work.

Studies on Hysteria occupies a unique place in psychoanalysis. When Breuer's and Freud's book was published in 1895, physicians had been baffled by the patients who came to them suffering from "nervous diseases." They had almost no useful theories to help them understand these individuals and no effective treatments. When C. G. Jung in Zurich, Wilhelm Stekel and Alfred Adler in Vienna, Sandor Ferenczi in Budapest, and others read *Studies*, it was an eye-opening experience. Here, finally, was a way of comprehending all the paralyses, tics, nervous coughs, mysterious pains, phobias, compulsions, obsessive thoughts, and nightmares they encountered in their patients. And not only understand them; *Studies* outlined a method of treatment that was like no other. These doctors immersed themselves in this book and its successor, *The Interpretation of Dreams*, and sought Freud out. Psychoanalysis, at first confined to a small group in Vienna, would eventually become a worldwide movement.

CHAPTER TWO

The Vision of a Heroic Self

Whatever principles he may reason from, and whatever logic he may follow, the philosopher is at bottom an advocate pleading to a brief handed over to his intellect by the peculiarities of his nature and the influences in his history that have molded his imagination.

WILLIAM JAMES
Manuscript Essays and Notes, 1903

When he was a boy, Freud envisioned himself in various heroic roles, most particularly as a military leader: Hannibal, Alexander the Great, Napoleon, Oliver Cromwell, Cortez. He imagined himself back in ancient times although, in fact, his early years were filled with enough adversity to make a child doubt his place in the world. His vision of a heroic self was a compensation for the poverty, failed father, losses, and anti-Semitism that filled his childhood.

In the first three and a half years of his life, Freud experienced a number of losses that were a major source of the anxiety that plagued him for many years. When he was less than a year old his mother, Amalia, gave birth to a son, who died approximately eight months later. He thus lost her care and affection, first to this infant and then to her grief over her dead child. Six more babies were born by the time he was ten, five sisters and a brother, reinforcing the impact of this first loss.

At age seventy-five Freud gave a striking description of a young child's reactions to such events; the links to his own life are obvious: "The child grudges the unwanted intruder and rival . . . all the other signs of maternal care. It feels that it has been dethroned, despoiled, damaged in its rights; it casts a jealous hatred upon the new baby and develops a grievance against the faithless mother."

But Freud then insisted that it is not he, or any male, who feels this way, only young girls. "A mother is only brought unlimited satisfaction by her relation to a son; this is altogether the most perfect, the most free from ambivalence of all human relationships." These passages show an awareness of the child's reaction to maternal loss and sibling rivals while simultaneously disavowing his own anxiety and anger. In reality, if not in his theoretical speculations, Freud felt a powerful ambivalence toward his mother: a great yearning for her love, anxiety and anger over losing her, and a need to control these potentially overwhelming emotions. In addition to the recurring losses of his mother's affection and attention to new babies, he also lost a vital substitute mother, his nursemaid, with whom he had a strong and loving bond. She was caught stealing from the family when he was two and a half years old and was sent to prison; she vanished abruptly from his life, and he never saw her again.

Further painful losses followed. When Freud was three and a half his father, Jacob, went bankrupt, and the family was forced to move away from the small town (Freiberg, about 150 miles north of Vienna) where he was born. The extended family was a complicated one; Jacob, over forty years old when Sigmund was born, was a widower with two grown sons from his first marriage, one of whom, Emmanuel, was himself married and the father of a son and daughter, who were Freud's age and his first playmates. All the family members worked together in Jacob's wool business. These half brothers, and Emmanuel's wife, were uncle and aunt figures to the young boy. Freud, his mother, his father, and his younger sister Anna moved—without the rest of the family—first to Leipzig, Germany, and then to Vienna, where they settled permanently. This move not only was an uprooting from the only home he had known, but also entailed the loss of his playmates and other family members. At the train station the young

Sigmund was overcome with fear that the train would leave without him, that he would lose the people he most needed. He remembered the gaslights in the station as "souls, burning in hell" (his nursemaid had taken him to Catholic mass) and no doubt cried in the large and bewildering place. This was the first appearance of a travel phobia that lasted all his life.

Jacob's business failure was a severe disappointment whose effects continued well into Freud's adulthood, because his father never got back on his feet financially, and the family lived on the brink of poverty for many years. They were forced to rely on money sent from England by Jacob's older sons, Amalia's relatives, and, later, from Eli Bernays, after he married Freud's sister Anna. When Freud himself was a struggling medical student, dependent on loans from friends, he sent small sums to the family to keep his other sisters from having to work as servants. As he wrote in a letter in his midforties, "I know from my youth that once the wild horses of the pampas have been lassoed, they retain a certain anxiousness for life. Thus, I came to know the helplessness of poverty and continually fear it."

When Freud was about five the family moved to Vienna, where they continued to live in close, cramped quarters, just as they had in Freiberg. All family activities took place in front of the young boy: his mother's and father's reactions to the death of his infant brother, their worries about the bankruptcy and poverty, parental sex, the births of additional babies, nursing, and the care of infants. He had no refuge from all these aspects of his life, including the six little children, who were constantly underfoot. In his later theories Freud stresses the anxiety a child supposedly feels when he or she witnesses, or even imagines, parental intercourse, the dreaded "primal scene." But his own family situation suggests that as a child he was exposed to far more disruptive and disturbing events than his parent's lovemaking.

The mild-mannered and somewhat humble Jacob was a financial failure, and his inability to support his family, along with his passive nature, led his son to reject him as a role model. In *The Interpretation of Dreams*, Freud recounts a story in which his father told him how a man once knocked Jacob's hat into the gutter and said, "Jew! Get off the pavement!" When his young son asked him what he did in response, Jacob said he meekly complied, whereupon Sigmund vowed to take the Carthaginian general Hannibal as his model. As he put it in his 1914 essay, *Some Reflections on Schoolboy Psychology,*

> The boy . . . cannot fail now to make discoveries which undermine his original high opinion of his father and which expedite his detachment from his first ideal. He finds that his father is no longer the mightiest, wisest and richest of beings; he grows dissatisfied with him, he learns to criticize him and to estimate his place in society; and then, as a rule, he makes him pay heavily for the disappointment that has been caused by him.

As Sigmund grew older, he tried to shut out the family clamor by withdrawing into the world of books. But he was not given his own room (a small, closetlike space where he read and studied) until he was nineteen years old and a student at the University of Vienna. Nevertheless, from early in his childhood Freud lived in his imagination; here he was a hero in worlds far away and long ago: ancient Egypt, Athenian Greece, and the Roman Empire. As he put it in the same essay,

> I used to find, the present time seemed to sink into obscurity and the years between ten and eighteen would rise from the corners of my memory, with all their guesses and illusions, their painful distortions and heartening successes—my first glimpses of an extinct civilization, which in my case was to bring me as much consolation as anything else in the struggles of life.

When he finally achieved success as an adult, Freud sought this same form of consolation in passionate collecting of artifacts from the ancient world. He would bring each new item he acquired to the midday family meal and look at and fondle it. The tables and cabinets of his Vienna office were filled to overflowing with these objects.

When the sixth child, his only brother, was born, a "family council" was called to decide the child's name. The ten-year-old Sigmund persuaded his parents to name the boy Alexander after the hero of the ancient world and gave a long recital of Alexander the Great's exploits. His identification with military heroes—Hannibal, Alexander, Napoleon, the conquistador Cortez, Oliver Cromwell—lasted all his life and foreshadowed his drive to become a world-famous scientist, his sweeping theoretical pronouncements, his style of therapy, and the way he shaped the psychoanalytic movement.

During the later years of his childhood Freud was a brilliant student and a controlling big brother. If his sisters were too openly emotional, for example when playing the piano, he made them stop. He also prohibited them from reading the novels of Balzac or Dumas, which he deemed too racy. Reading and studying seemed to fill the greatest part of his own time. His sister Anna described his male friends as "study mates," and there is almost no sense of play, fun, or boyish pranks; he was a premature adult. The world of language, books, study, and his imagination was a safe refuge from the emotional turmoil of the family—the frightening losses, poverty, his dominating mother and weak father, the feminine world of mother and the many little sisters—and it set up a pattern in which emotion of all kinds was subordinated to reading, the privacy of his imagination, and, later, writing.

Many who have described Freud's childhood picture it as a happy time when he was the favored child, his mother's "Golden Sigi," the precocious, high-achieving, first-born son. It is true that his mother treated him as special, which reinforced his identification with the heroic figures whom he idolized during his formative years. But being singled out in this way was a mixed blessing. His parents, especially his mother, valued him for his performance, for the way in which his accomplishments would reflect on them. In the oft-quoted phrase "My Golden Sigi," the emphasis should be on the "My." Although Freud, in his theory of the Oedipus complex, promoted the father to the position of power in what he termed "the family romance," within his own family Amalia was the dominant figure. Freud's oldest son Martin described his grandmother as "highly emotional, easily carried away by her feelings . . . not easy to live with. . . . She had great vitality and much impatience; she had a hunger for life and an indomitable spirit." Freud's niece, who lived with the family for a time, described her as "shrill and domineering . . . charming and smiling when strangers were about, but . . . with familiars she was a tyrant, and a selfish one." As an old woman Amalia remained vain and demanding, and her son, even when over seventy, still got a stomachache every time he went to see her at the obligatory weekly family meal. He wrote of his great sense of personal freedom after her death at age ninety-five.

The centrality of the defenses Freud created by his emotional withdrawal into the world of language and his imagination can be seen in the most important relationships of his later life: that with his adolescent best friend, Eduard Silberstein; the long courtship of his fiancée, Martha Bernays; his intimacy with Wilhelm Fliess; and his close relationship with C. G. Jung. All these relationships were conducted by letter with people who lived in distant cities. Intellectual control through language and writing are also the precursors to the theories that abound in his psychoanalytic books and essays, a largely private world filled with theoretical speculations and terms of his own invention. This control also anticipates psychoanalytic treatment, in which disruptive emotional states are to be mastered by interpretation—delivered by an analyst who is out of sight behind the couch—and intellectual insight.

The period from Freud's late childhood until his midtwenties was an extended "adolescent moratorium," to use the culturally oriented psychoanalyst Erik Erikson's concept: a time when adult goals—an intimate sexual relationship, the assumption of responsibilities, and family—were postponed. He worked hard at his studies; did extremely well in the Gymnasium or secondary school, mastering several languages; and did well at the University of Vienna, where he eventually settled on a medical-scientific course of study. Following graduation he went to work as an assistant in the laboratory of the physiologist Ernst Brücke, one of several outstanding scientists at the university.

Brücke was a new hero for the young man to idolize, a famous scientist and demanding teacher, as well as someone with tight control over his emotions. Freud referred to his professor as "the great Brücke" and "Master Brücke," and called him "the greatest authority I ever met," an opinion that never changed. He spoke of his time at the Physiology Institute as the happiest years of his student days. Brücke's extreme emotional control was quite clear to Freud after the former's beloved son died. He forbade anyone to mention the son's name, put away all pictures of him, and focused on his work even more than before. His stature as a scientist, and his austerity and self-control, all powerfully influenced Freud, who at this time dealt with his own potentially troubling emotions with restraint and endless hard work. The kind of research Freud performed has been described as "a school of scientific asceticism and self-denial," involving long and arduous hours hunched over the microscope, teasing out nerve fibers, developing methods for displaying them, and writing carefully done scientific papers. He was most comfortable in his labors in the physiology laboratory and friendships with men. As he later put it, "in Brücke's physiological laboratory, I found rest and full satisfaction—and men, too, whom I could respect and take as my models."

Freud had no contact with members of the opposite sex throughout these years. He was decidedly shy and afraid of women and was a virgin when he married at age thirty. Vienna was not a prudish Victorian city, and many men of his class and education, such as the writer Arthur Schnitzler (see his *My Life in Vienna*), visited prostitutes and carried on affairs with women from a variety of social classes. The fact that Freud waited until his marriage to become sexually active reveals the extent of his inhibitions.

Toward the end of his time as Brücke's assistant, Freud was granted a travel fellowship to study in Paris with the famous neurologist Jean-Martin Charcot, known then as "The Napoleon of Neuroses." Charcot gave demonstrations in his clinic—to which members of the French intelligentsia were invited—in which he showed how "hysterical" patients could be hypnotized and their symptoms made to appear and disappear. Such demonstrations showed the lack of a physical basis for the symptoms and were striking evidence of unconscious states of mind. However, Charcot had no meaningful theory about the cause of hysteria, attributing it to "hereditary degeneracy," and no useful therapeutic methods. He would treat his patients with electrical stimulation or the ingestion of iron, or by hanging them from the ceiling in iron harnesses. Nevertheless, Freud was impressed by the flamboyant Frenchman, who became another scientist-hero in his pantheon.

Throughout his early twenties Freud was a compliant, hard-working student and budding scientist, who was rewarded by his professors for his careful research. His work progressed from microscopic anatomy to clinical neurology and, finally, to theoretical neurology, as seen in *On Aphasia*, published when he was thirty-five. He was not in the least rebellious and did not seem to suffer much of the anxiety and depression that so troubled him later. His fears, anger, and dreams of heroism were all submerged and channeled into his work, which gave him a sense of accomplishment, earned him praise, and provided order and structure to his life. His identification with Brücke allowed him to feel strong and calm; he, too, could become a famous scientist, not troubled by emotional turmoil. But his need for love remained unfulfilled.

At age twenty-six he met a young woman, Martha Bernays, who was visiting his sisters, and was immediately taken with her; it was love at first sight. He broke out of his extended adolescent moratorium, proposed marriage to Martha just a few months after their first meeting, and began a long engagement. Eventually he was advised by Brücke that if he wished to begin a family, he had best leave his position in the laboratory—where a promotion was unlikely and he would never earn much money—and consider entering private medical practice. This he did, opening his own office with a specialty in neurology shortly after his marriage.

Freud's relationship with Martha from the very beginning reveals the different sides of his personality. Martha was a slight, shy woman, four years his junior, whose father had died shortly before their first meeting. The Bernays had been a solid middle-class family, but the father's death left them in a precarious financial position. She was an obedient daughter, devoted to her Orthodox Jewish mother, and did not question the repressive sexual mores imposed on women of her class and time. Shortly after their engagement Martha's mother moved the family to a town outside of Hamburg, Germany, their original home. Because he was too poor to get married sooner, for over four years Freud's principal contact with his fiancée was by letter. He wrote almost every day, pouring out his love and need for her. He was prone to powerful jealousy of potential rivals, including a previous suitor, her mother, and her older brother Eli, a generous and outgoing former friend of Sigmund's. He picked fights with both her mother and Eli over trivial matters and insisted that Martha side with him, tearing her away from her beloved family members, who were now, in his words, "enemies." These fights were unconscious remnants of his reactions to all those sisters who took his mother from him as a child; this time he would prevail, he would have the woman's love entirely for himself. His behavior also reveals his need to dominate, which later came to the fore in his position as leader of the psychoanalytic movement.

Freud was not only jealous, he was afraid he would lose Martha to sickness or death. He would express concern if his letters were not answered immediately, a pattern that continued throughout his life with his close male friends. When he loved someone, fear of loss and the urgent longing for contact were powerfully activated. His excessive concern with Martha's health also had its roots in his childhood. When Sigmund was a boy, Amalia periodically suffered from tuberculosis, the great scourge of the nineteenth century. In *The Interpretation of Dreams*, he reports the memory of a frightening nightmare he had when he was eight, in which he saw his mother's dead body. He recalled that he "awoke in tears and screaming, and interrupted my parents sleep. . . . I remembered that I suddenly grew calm when I saw my mother's face, as though I needed to be reassured that she was not dead."

Freud required a submissive partner. Throughout the correspondence he refers to his darling "Marty." as "sweet," "innocent," and his "Little Princess." Petite, with little money, and unassuming, she was the anti-Amalia. He could have sought out someone who was emancipated and freethinking, but he was never attracted to any woman who might be his equal. He also insisted that their six children be named after people important to him, although they could have followed Jewish custom—which was very important to Martha, who had been raised in an orthodox home—by naming their oldest son after her recently deceased father. Freud named their first son Jean Martin, after Charcot; the third son Ernst, after Brücke; and the second son Oliver, after Oliver Cromwell, the aggressive general who won the English Civil War. This last choice must have been particularly puzzling to his wife. In addition, he chose their apartment without consulting her and made her give up all religious practices. Martha later commented on "how not being allowed to light the Sabbath lights on the first Friday night after her marriage was one of the more upsetting experiences of her life."

Freud's demand that Martha remain in the subordinate role of wife and mother was already apparent during their engagement, when he told her about his disagreement with John Stuart Mill's ideas about the rights of women. He had earned some money by translating a few of Mill's essays into German, and wrote to his fiancée, "It seems a completely unrealistic notion to send women into the struggle for existence in the same way as men. Am I to think of my delicate sweet girl as a competitor? . . . The position of woman cannot be other than what it is: to be an adored sweetheart in youth and a beloved wife in maturity." And so it was; Martha largely subordinated herself to his wishes, and he successfully imposed his will on her.

Martha took on the role of supportive wife and devoted mother of the children. She and her unmarried sister Minna, who joined the family after the untimely death of her fiancé, ran everything at home. They were referred to as "Siamese twins"; Freud called them "the two mothers" who ruled the household. Martha did manage to carve out one area of independence from Freud's control, showing no interest in what came to be the great passion of his life, psychoanalysis. As she put it, "I must admit that if I did not realize how seriously my husband takes his treatments, I should think that psychoanalysis is a form of pornography!" The roots of his treatment of his female patients, and his theories about femininity, can be seen in the ideas about women that he expressed to Martha, as well as in their marriage.

Despite making himself an absolute monarch at home, Freud still regarded sexual intimacy with a woman as dangerous. Although he never publicly wrote about his marriage, the most revealing picture of it can be found in his 1908 essay, "'Civilized' Sexual Morality and Modern Nervous Illness":

This brings us to the question whether sexual intercourse in legal marriage can offer full compensation for the restriction imposed before marriage. There is such an abundance of material supporting a reply in the negative that we can give only the briefest summary of it. It must above all be borne in mind that our cultural sexual morality restricts sexual intercourse even in marriage itself, since it imposes on married couples the necessity of contenting themselves, as a rule, with a very few procreative acts. As a consequence of this consideration, satisfying sexual intercourse in marriage takes place only for a few years; and we must subtract from this, of course, the intervals of abstention necessitated by regard for the wife's health. After these three, four or five years, the marriage becomes a failure in so far as it has promised the satisfaction of sexual needs. For all the devices hitherto invented for preventing conception impair sexual enjoyment, hurt the fine susceptibilities of both partners and even actually cause illness. Fear of the consequences of sexual intercourse first brings the married couple's physical affection to an end; and then, as a remoter result, it usually puts a stop as well to the mental sympathy between them, which should have been the succession to their original passionate love. The spiritual disillusionment and bodily deprivation to which most marriages are thus doomed puts both partners back in the state they were in before their marriage, except for being the poorer by the loss of an illusion, and they must once more have recourse to their fortitude in mastering and deflecting their sexual instinct.

These comments have been taken as Freud's doleful insights on the difficulties of finding happiness in marriage rather than as a disguised account of his relationship with his wife. When he speaks of contraceptive devices hurting "the fine susceptibilities of both partners and even actually causing illness," what is he referring to? Condoms were used by men with prostitutes to protect themselves against disease, so in his mind, to use one might make his wife feel soiled. His friends and colleagues—many of whom were physicians—as well as others who shared his nonreligious, scientific outlook, seemed to have no difficulty practicing birth control, however. His concern for "the wife's health" and the odd idea that using contraception can cause illness has no basis in reality, though the notion later crept into some of his theories on the role of sexuality in neurosis.

Freud's sexual interest in Martha declined during the early years of the marriage; the ardent embraces and kisses of the engagement disappeared. In several of his letters to friends, he alluded to his lack of sexual activity, impotence, or inability to obtain pleasure. At the age of forty-one he wrote to his closest friend, Wilhelm Fliess, "Sexual excitement, too, is no longer of use for someone like me." Thirteen years later he wrote to Jung, then his favorite disciple, "My Indian summer of eroticism that we spoke of on our trip has withered lamentably under the pressure of work." And later still, he told his American colleague, James J. Putnam, "I stand for an infinitely freer sexual life, although I myself have made very little use of such freedom."

One cause of his loss of sexual interest after the first few years of marriage may have been the pregnancies and arrival of new babies, which occurred with great rapidity; six children were born in eight years. When the slim girl of the courtship became a mother-to-be, it no doubt set off the unconscious fear of loss associated with his own mother's pregnancies, as well as his anger at being displaced by rivals for her love and attention. As if anticipating this, he wrote to Martha two years before their wedding, "I always think that once one is married one no longer—in most cases—lives for each other as one used to. One lives rather with each other for some third thing, and for the husband dangerous rivals soon appear: household and nursery."

For all his psychoanalytic insight, Freud never saw the disappointments of his own marriage as due to his and Martha's personal characteristics. In the essay "'Civilized' Sexual Morality," he attributed the failure of intimacy to outside factors such as contraception and "cultural sexual morality." There certainly were social taboos that interfered with sexual pleasure: feelings of shame or a sense of guilt arising from a punitive conscience. Freud's insights into these factors were eventually liberating for many people, though not for him. But not everyone in his time was held back by such restrictions, and by framing his discussion in terms of general taboos, he avoided examining the powerful emotional inhibitions from which he and Martha suffered.

His letters to Martha during their engagement mentioned many of the novels he was reading, including Henry Fielding's ribald *Tom Jones*, though he "did not think it suitable for her chaste mind." His inhibitions were not confined to sexuality, but extended to other emotion-laden activities as well. As a boy and adolescent, he needed to control the excitement, joy, and sadness aroused by music, not only in himself but in those around him. Freud's aversion to music was well known to his colleagues, and Ernest Jones recalled, "the pained expression on his face on entering a restaurant or beer garden where there was a band and how quickly his hands would go over his ears to drown the sound."

Vienna at the end of the nineteenth century was alive with exciting new developments in painting, in the works of Gustave Klimt and others; in music, in the compositions of Mahler; in architecture; and in revolutionary social and political ideas. All this seemed to pass Freud by, immersed as he was in his mind and the world of ancient artifacts. He wrote to Martha, after seeing the opera *Carmen*, about the way the two of them differed from common people, or "the rabble," as he later referred to them:

> The mob gives vent to its appetites, and we deprive ourselves. We deprive ourselves in order to maintain our integrity, we economize in our health, our capacity for enjoyment, our emotions; we save ourselves for something, not knowing what. And this habit of constant suppression of natural instincts gives us the quality of refinement.

In the end, the two of them lived together in what appeared to be relative contentment, but it is clear that after the romantic courtship of the letters, his real passions were directed elsewhere. Martha was, as he remarked to his disciple, Marie Bonaparte, many years later, "not a bad solution of the marriage problem."

Leaving Brücke's laboratory and getting married set loose disturbing emotions in Freud. As his biographer, Ernest Jones, never one to cast a negative light on his idol, notes,

> There is ample evidence that for ten years or so—roughly compris-
> ing the nineties—he suffered from a very considerable psychoneuro-
> sis. . . . His sufferings were at times very intense, and for those ten
> years there could have been only occasional intervals when life
> seemed much worth living. . . . It consisted essentially in extreme
> changes of mood, and the only respects in which the anxiety got lo-
> calized were occasional attacks of dread of dying . . . and anxiety
> about traveling by rail. . . . The alternations of mood were between
> periods of elation, excitement, and self-confidence on the one hand
> and periods of severe depression, doubt, and inhibition on the other.
> In the depressed moods he could neither write nor concentrate his
> thoughts. . . . He would spend leisure hours of extreme boredom,
> turning from one thing to another, cutting open books, looking at
> maps of ancient Pompeii, playing patience or chess, but being unable
> to continue at anything for long—a state of restless paralysis. Some-
> times there were spells where consciousness would be greatly nar-
> rowed: states, difficult to describe, with a veil that produced almost a
> twilight condition of mind.

Freud's severe anxiety and depression, with the specific symptoms of fear of dying and the travel phobia (both of which lasted, in attenuated forms, all his life), were all related to the traumatic losses of his earliest years. He even attempted to escape these painful emotions by returning to the imaginative world of his childhood, such as when he looked "at maps of ancient Pompeii." Since his marriage had not succeeded in giving him the love and understanding he needed to overcome the disruptive states de-scribed by Jones—it was rather, as he poignantly put it, "the loss of an il-lusion"—he turned in other directions for relief.

During his engagement to Martha, Freud had begun experimenting with cocaine. He thought he would find medical uses for it that would bring him fame, but also took the drug to counter his "migraines," depression, and other disruptive emotional states. He spoke of how cocaine would lift him out of his withdrawn condition, making him feel more confident and energetic, and he continued to rely on it for a number of years. His addiction to nicotine—which produces similar, if shorter lasting, effects—lasted all his life; he smoked about twenty cigars a day.

Freud also sought out intimate relationships with men. Even before his marriage he had an erotically tinged connection with an older, brilliant colleague, Ernst Fleischl von Marxow. Fleischl had become addicted to morphine, which he took to relieve the intractable pain of an injury. Freud tried to cure him of his dependence by giving him cocaine, only to have his friend become addicted to this drug as well. He wrote to Martha, "I admire and love him with an intellectual passion, if you will allow such a phrase. His destruction will move me as the destruction of a sacred and famous temple would have affected an ancient Greek." He and Fleischl would spend whole nights together, with his friend taking drugs, and Freud sitting beside his bath. He wrote, "I ask myself if I shall ever in my life experience anything so agitating or exciting as these nights . . . his talk, his explanations of all possible obscure things . . . his manifold activity interrupted by states of the completest exhaustion relieved by morphia and cocaine: all that makes an ensemble that cannot be described." He kept a photograph of Fleischl over the couch in his consulting room for the rest of his life. In the years before and immediately after his marriage, he became involved with two men who were to play very significant roles in his life, Josef Breuer and Wilhelm Fliess.

It is difficult to think of people as living simultaneously on several different levels, as having disparate sides of themselves. We like our heroes and leaders, especially, to be completely virtuous, brilliant, and powerful; evil, stupidity, and weakness are reserved for "others." And yet we should know that people are more complex, that there are entire sides of themselves about which they are not aware. If we wish to fully comprehend psychoanalysis, this is how we must see Freud: the discoverer of the unconscious who was, at the same time, unaware of many of his own motives; the greatest psychological theorist of the twentieth century, whose doctrines were often wrong; the man who developed a strikingly new method of treatment while at the same time encumbering it with rules that made it less than therapeutic. Freud's personality had many dimensions. In his earliest years he was a frightened young child. But these fears went underground as he became a brilliant and diligent student who, in his private fantasy world, harbored heroic aspirations. Later he was a dutiful apprentice to the famous Brücke, admired the Napoleonic Charcot, and became a budding neurologist, attempting to work with a bewildering array of patients.

CHAPTER THREE

A Scientist Treats the Passions

Great scientists have an instinct for the fruitful and doable, particularly for smaller questions that lead on and eventually transform the grand issues from speculation to action. . . . Great theories must sink a huge anchor in details.
STEPHEN JAY GOULD
The New York Review of Books, 1986

*F*reud had few social connections and no family money. This vulnerable position amplified his lifelong desire to have an accomplished older man lend him strength as he embarked on his new professional career. Nine years before his marriage to Martha, while he was still an assistant in Brücke's Physiological Institute, he first met Josef Breuer, who would come to fill this role. Breuer, fourteen years older than Freud, was an established physician who also had independent scientific interests. Within a few years their relationship flowered, and the older man became an intimate friend, advisor, mentor, and benefactor to the novice doctor, whose potential brilliance he sensed. Throughout the 1880s and early 1890s they became very close, sharing professional and personal confidences. All of this led to the joint publication of *Studies on Hysteria* in 1895.

Breuer and Freud were similar in a number of ways. Both were Viennese Jews, trained at the University of Vienna Medical School, one of the leading medical-scientific centers in the world at that time. They were not religious but were imbued with the rational-scientific ethos of the era, though they nonetheless suffered from the anti-Semitism so prevalent in the Austro-Hungarian Empire. Perhaps most significant, they were both extremely original and creative in their work.

However, there were significant differences between them that presaged the eventual break in their relationship. Breuer was materially comfortable, whereas Freud still struggled to make a living. Breuer had made very valuable scientific discoveries, was one of the most respected internists and family physicians in Vienna, yet was extraordinarily modest and not at all interested in fame. Early in his life he knew that he wanted to be a physician, and he was devoted to the care of his patients and the advancement of scientific knowledge. Freud, by his own admission, was never strongly motivated to become a doctor. As he wrote in the *Autobiographical Study* he published in 1925, "Neither at that time, nor indeed in my later life, did I feel any particular predilection for the career of a doctor. I was moved, rather, by a sort of curiosity, which was, however, directed more towards human concerns than towards natural objects." In 1920 he admitted to a patient in analysis, "I have no great interest in therapeutic problems. I am much too impatient now. . . . I am too much occupied with theoretical problems all the time, so that whenever I get occasion, I am working on my own theoretical problems, rather than paying attention to the therapeutic problems." As time passed, it became clear that his primary goal was to create a theory that would make him famous—a goal he pursued above all else.

Josef Breuer was born in 1842 into a family at the opposite end of the social and economic spectrum from Freud's. His father, Leopold, to whom he remained devoted, began life as a poor rabbinical student but married into a prosperous family of merchants, became a well-known religious teacher, and adopted modern ideas. He and his wife were part of the established, well-educated, cultured Jewish Viennese community. Breuer's mother Bertha died when he was three, following the birth of his younger brother. Thus, like Freud, he suffered an early maternal loss. But it was Breuer's good fortune that his grandmother, a brilliant and witty woman, took over management of the household and cared for Josef and his brother. Unlike Freud, Breuer had a successful father whom he could look up to during his childhood. Although he lost his mother, his grandmother seemed to be a loving substitute, and he was free from the distress of being replaced by an endless stream of babies. Apparently there was nothing comparable to the "Golden Sigi" period of Freud's life; Josef was not put in the position of having to satisfy a parent's ambitions.

Breuer remembered his early years as "on the whole . . . very tranquil, very happy and peaceful." As an adult he did not have to depend on friends for handouts, as Freud did for many years. There were temperamental differences between the two men as well. Breuer was easygoing and sociable, with a large circle of friends. He seemed comfortable with himself, whereas Freud could become locked up in the private world of his mind, struggling for control and filled with conflicting emotions. When he was twenty-four years old, Breuer married Matilda Altmann, a woman from an affluent family, further cementing his financial security.

His position and skills brought him many prominent people as patients, including members of the University Medical School faculty such as Brücke and Fleischl. He was both doctor to and friend of many of the members of Vienna's most distinguished families, who valued the combination of scientific-medical knowledge and his personal qualities: warmth, understanding, and generosity. Breuer also treated a number of destitute patients at no cost or for very low fees.

In addition to his large medical practice, Breuer conducted original research in several areas, motivated by the quest for scientific understanding. He pursued this work in the evenings, often in collaboration with other investigators. He made his most original contributions in three areas: the transmission of wound fever, the regulation of respiration, and the function of the labyrinth or inner ear in balance. His experiments on wounds and infections established that fever was transmitted in the bloodstream and not via nerve fibers, as some thought at the time. His research on respiration was carried out in collaboration with Ewald Hering. Together they discovered the role of the vagus nerve in the frequency, depth, and rhythm of breathing. In this work he used an early version of what is now known as an information-feedback model of the nervous system, a theory far ahead of its time. Medical students today still learn about the Hering-Breuer reflex. His study of the function of the inner ear or aural labyrinth was of great complexity and occupied him for many years. His findings coincided with those of the physicist Ernst Mach and became known as the "Mach-Breuer flow theory of the vestibular apparatus." His scientific findings in all these areas, with some minor modifications, remain valid today.

Breuer's strengths as a scientist were apparent in all of this research. He selected an important question that needed to be answered, devised and carried out incisive experiments, and interpreted his findings in creative and sophisticated ways. His biological views were ahead of their time, and he was careful, committed to observation and evidence, and not given to sweeping speculations. He had a deep distaste for dogmatism and did not accept ideas on the basis of authority. He was not opposed to theoretical speculation when it was required, but maintained a skeptical stance until he was persuaded by evidence. Nor did he cultivate the aura of a charismatic authority. He adopted as his motto Spinoza's *suum esse conservare*, "to preserve one's own essence," and was a man of great personal and scientific integrity. His letters reveal an individual who was a "stalwart critic of every injustice, the accuser of corruption and gossip, the vigorous opponent of nationalist and racist excesses."

In addition to his outstanding work as a practicing physician and his scientific contributions, Breuer was very knowledgeable about literature, art, politics, and history, both ancient and modern. He corresponded with philosophers such as Franz Brentano, one of Freud's undergraduate teachers, and many others, about the scientific, philosophical, and cultural issues of the day. In spite of his accomplishments, he was known for his "excessive modesty."

Freud, at the beginning of his medical career, could not have found a better friend and mentor than Breuer. The two men spent time together in the evenings, discussing scientific as well as personal matters, including the women in their lives. Freud was a frequent visitor to the Breuer home and was also friends with Matilda Breuer. He dedicated *On Aphasia*—a careful scientific work that brilliantly synthesized the neurology of the time and pointed the way to future developments—to Breuer in 1891, and named his first daughter Matilda. Breuer never played the role of distant authority like Brücke or Charcot; he encouraged Freud's independence, pushing him to realize his potential in his own way. He also enriched Freud's understanding of philosophy, literature, and art.

For several years Breuer gave the impoverished Freud a monthly stipend, a "loan" that he did not expect would be repaid. When Freud expressed discomfort about accepting the money, Breuer told him that he could easily afford it and that Freud, rather than losing self-respect, should take the gift as an indication of his value in the world. Breuer would sometimes take Freud on his medical rounds, and when these took them to distant cities where they spent the night, the older man would sign Freud into the hotel as his brother so that he would not have to leave his own tip. These acts reveal Breuer's generosity and exquisite sensitivity to Freud's feelings about his poverty. As Freud once wrote to his fiancée, to talk with Breuer was "like sitting in the sun. . . . He radiates light and warmth. . . . He is such a sunny person, and I don't know what he sees in me to be so kind. . . . He is a man who always understands one."

Breuer was also Freud's main source of patient referrals, essential to establishing a medical practice. His greatest gift to his young friend, however, was the description of his work with Bertha Pappenheim, a "hysterical" young woman whom he treated in 1880–1882. He saw Bertha before the height of his friendship with Freud, and his therapy with her was the true beginning of psychoanalysis. She appears as the first case in the book they later published together, *Studies on Hysteria.*

As a physician with a large practice, Breuer saw patients suffering from a wide variety of diseases, including many who were labeled hysterics. The diagnosis was applied to patients (mainly women) who displayed a number of mystifying symptoms, including general states of anxiety and depression; alterations in consciousness, including amnesia, divided or split consciousness, and multiple selves; and physical symptoms such as paralyses, headaches, pain, anesthesia, deafness, blindness, convulsions, anorexia, and nervous coughs. Despite the best efforts of many medical specialists, no physical bases could be found for most of these symptoms. They peri-odically appeared and disappeared, which would not have occurred if ac-tual neurological damage were present. Physicians could not agree on the diagnosis, and many speculated about physical factors such as anatomical lesions, spinal cord damage, and "instability" or "over-excitation" of the nervous system—hence the general name "neurosis" and the reason many of these patients were referred to neurologists like Freud. There was no agreement on what "hysteria" was or what caused it, and no clearly estab-lished treatment.

A current view is that hysteria was a condition mainly found in the nineteenth century, perhaps related to the sexual repression of women. However, a close look at the actual cases in *Studies* and elsewhere reveals that this idea is not supported by the evidence. Many of the patients la-beled hysteric suffered from severe post-traumatic conditions, overwhelm-ing loss of loved ones, frustrating identity struggles—especially in a culture that placed enormous restrictions on women—and disturbed in-terpersonal relationships. Some would now be diagnosed as suffering from post-traumatic stress disorder, multiple personality, borderline personality disorder, bipolar disorder, and even schizophrenia, and others may have had neurological conditions that were unknown at the time. In short, the answer to the question "What was hysteria?" is that it never existed. "Hys-teria" was a grab bag diagnosis; there was never a single disease or condi-tion, analogous to tuberculosis or syphilis, so there could never be one explanation or cure for it.

Nevertheless, physicians like Breuer struggled to understand these deeply troubled patients and tried to find ways to help them. A variety of treatments were in vogue, including special diets and medications. Some of the drugs were relatively harmless, such as iron and bromine, whereas others, such as morphine, chloral hydrate, and chloroform, were quite powerful and addictive. Exercise regimes and trips to spas and the moun-tains or seashore were popular options. But the two most common treat-ments were Erb's electrotherapy and the Weir Mitchell method. In Erb's method, a mild (and sometimes not so mild) electrical current was applied to afflicted parts of the body, producing tingling sensations and muscle spasms. The Weir Mitchell treatment involved a combination of isolation, bed rest, massage, electrical stimulation, and a strict diet. An astute physician like Breuer could see that none of these treatments produced lasting cures; what benefits the patients did derive were probably from a placebo effect, though this was not known at the time. Although some of these methods produced temporary results, they shed no light on the cause of the condition, nor did they lead to treatments with lasting results.

This was the situation when Breuer began to experiment with hypnotism as a method of treating hysterical patients. Hypnotism itself had had a checkered history over the preceding century, being associated with stage performers and charlatans. But there were also legitimate scientists who had demonstrated its uses, including Charcot, whose work Freud had witnessed in 1885. Some of the symptoms of hysteria, such as anesthesia, paralyses, and amnesia, could be induced and removed in patients through hypnotic suggestion, which was employed in Charcot's dramatic demonstrations. Breuer was aware of the work of Charcot; the French physician Bernheim, who used hypnotism in the treatment of hysteria; and several others, including his and Freud's mutual friend, Fleischl. He was also aware of the connection between some hysterical symptoms and trauma. With the growth of rail travel, there were more train wrecks, and some of the people who had gone through such frightening experiences developed hysterical symptoms: so-called "railway spine" and "railway brain," in which the symptoms mimicked those found in spinal cord or brain injuries, though no physical damage could be discovered. Hypnotism had a natural appeal for working with these individuals, because it could produce alterations in consciousness, which were often part of the overall symptom picture. It was this combination of factors that led Breuer—always open to new treatment possibilities, even if they were controversial—to employ hypnotism with the young woman whom he began to treat in 1880, Bertha Pappenheim.

The Talking Cure:
Josef Breuer and Anna O.

You are not a woman, you may try but you can never imagine what it is to have a man's force of genius in you, and yet to suffer the slavery of being a girl. To have a pattern cut out—"this is the Jewish woman"—this is what you must be; this is what you are wanted for, a woman's heart must be of such a size and no larger or it must be pressed small, like Chinese feet; her happiness is to be made as cakes are, by a fixed recipe.

GEORGE ELIOT
Daniel Deronda, 1878

Bertha Pappenheim was a Jewish Viennese woman, interestingly enough a friend of Martha Freud, who had a "hysterical" break-down at the age of twenty-one. Josef Breuer was the family physician called in to treat her in 1880; he became very involved in her case, trying hypnosis and then a method that Bertha herself called "the talking cure" or "chimney sweeping." He called it "catharsis," a treatment in which he encouraged her to give full expression to all thoughts and feelings associated with her symptoms. Breuer treated her until 1882 and, when he and Freud were close friends in the late 1880s, described the case to his younger colleague, who was so intrigued that he asked him to go over the details a number of times. Freud then adopted Breuer's cathartic method with a series of his own patients, making modifications as he went along, until it eventually became psychoanalysis. Bertha appears as the first case, under the pseudonym "Anna O.," in *Studies on Hysteria*, which they published together in 1895. She was thus the first psychoanalytic patient, and Breuer's cathartic method was the real beginning of psychoanalysis as a theory and therapy.

When Breuer initially saw Bertha, she was suffering from a variety of extremely painful and serious symptoms. As far as her mother and brother could see, she had taken to her bed after nursing her dying father and was behaving in strange, if not bizarre, ways. She showed different states of consciousness that alternated frequently and without warning. In one condition she was relatively coherent, though sad and anxious; in the other she was "naughty" and abusive. Eventually, as she came to trust him, she confided her experiences exclusively to Breuer. She spoke of "having two selves, a real one and an evil one which forced her to behave badly." Amnesia was frequent and she sometimes suffered what she called "absences" during the day, when she was in a state of self-imposed or autohypnosis, and in the evening, when she was in a state she called "clouds" and could communicate more clearly. She also displayed striking changes of mood: "excessive but quite temporary high spirits and at other times severe anxiety, stubborn opposition to every therapeutic effort and frightening hallucinations of black snakes, which was how she saw her hair, ribbons and similar things." Powerful anxiety was the dominant emotion, along with suicidal urges and depression. She had to be moved to the ground floor of the house to prevent her throwing herself out of a window from an upper floor, where she had originally been kept.

Bertha also suffered from a bewildering variety of physical symptoms. She had partial paralysis ("contractures") of her legs, arms, and neck muscles, which made it difficult, and at times impossible, to rotate her head or use her limbs. She had severe headaches, facial pain, and disturbances of vision. Deafness and mutism came and went, and a nervous cough led to hoarseness and difficulty talking. Anorexia and other difficulties with food were part of the picture as well. For periods of time she could not speak in her native German, instead attempting to communicate in a mixture of four other languages. For some time she only spoke English.

Breuer's examination, as well as those of several specialists, found no physical bases for these symptoms, and he concluded that he had a severe case of "hysterical psychosis" on his hands. Although one can only guess about his motivation to help her, there were probably two principal reasons: his wish to alleviate the suffering of this intelligent and promising young woman, and his scientific curiosity. How could he make sense of this puzzling mass of symptoms and mental states? Perhaps his drive to help Bertha Pappenheim, who had just suffered the death of a parent, was also due to the arousal of emotions associated with the loss of the first Bertha in his life, his mother, who died when he was three years old. He certainly poured his heart and soul into Bertha's treatment: "His commitment to the case of Anna O. had been of an unusually high degree. . . . [His initial] report is ten or twenty times longer than usual for that period. An extraordinary degree of empathy is apparent from the case history."

Not a great deal is known about Bertha's childhood, but Breuer reported what he could about her family background. Because of his long and sympathetic involvement with her—in his own words, her "life became known to me to an extent to which one person's life is seldom known to another"—he is an excellent source of information, as are her own fantasies, the stories and poems she later wrote, and the career she pursued after her recovery.

The Pappenheims were a wealthy family, and as a young girl Bertha led a materially comfortable existence. Despite their wealth, she found her life stultifying. Her father was one of the founders of a synagogue, and he required his family to adhere to the strict rules of Orthodox Judaism. Bertha was groomed to be a good Jewish wife, studying Hebrew and biblical texts, prayers and rituals, and dietary restrictions, with special attention given to menstrual hygiene. She was also made to embroider her trousseau in preparation for marriage. She was given some secular education until the age of sixteen, studying literature, foreign languages, piano, and needlework, with the aim of giving her a patina of culture. But, as she wrote much later, this existence—riding, going for walks, tea parties, visits to the theater, doing handiwork, "producing those countless pointless, insipid trivia which prove so alarmingly durable precisely because of their uselessness"—was nothing more than a way to pass the time. Clearly she had far too much energy and intelligence for the life that was prescribed for her. As Breuer noted,

> She was markedly intelligent, with an astonishingly quick grasp of things and penetrating intuition. She possessed a powerful intellect which would have been capable of digesting solid mental pabulum and which stood in need of it—though without receiving it after she had left school. She had great poetic and imaginative gifts, which were under the control of a sharp and critical common sense. . . . Her will-power was energetic, tenacious and persistent; sometimes it reached the pitch of an obstinacy which only gave way out of kindness and regard for other people. One of her essential character traits was sympathetic kindness. Even during her illness she herself was greatly assisted by being able to look after a number of poor, sick people for she was thus able to satisfy a powerful instinct.

Not only did Bertha chafe under the constraints of her orthodox upbringing and the sterile existence assigned to women, but the family had also been scarred by death. Bertha was the third of four children; the two sisters who preceded her both died, the first six years before she was born, and the second when she was eight. Her younger brother went to the university and became a successful lawyer. As was typical at that time, the brilliant Bertha was denied the higher education she clearly needed, while her brother was encouraged to pursue a professional career. Her mother, in Breuer's words, was "a very solemn person" who was "displeased" by her surviving daughter's "gaiety." It is possible that Bertha's mother was depressed by the deaths of her two other children and emotionally unavailable to her lively and intelligent third girl. Breuer reported that there was conflict and discord between them.

Bertha turned to her father as a source of intellectual stimulation and love and focused her desires on him, to the exclusion of other men. As Breuer wrote in his initial report of 1883, "The sexual element is astonishingly undeveloped; I have never once found it represented even amongst her numerous hallucinations. At all events, she has never been in love to the extent that this has replaced her relationship to her father; it has itself, rather, been replaced by that relationship." This is a very interesting observation, suggesting that Bertha's father was the only source of her interest and affection, in contrast to her "solemn" mother. Yet this same father imposed the religious constraints on his daughter, the demand that she devote herself to preparations to be a "good" girl and future wife. One would assume that she felt a powerful ambivalence toward him that could find no open expression in this conventional family, and she became increasingly oblivious to her essential self. Outwardly she complied with all the family requirements and inwardly she rebelled. To Bertha, religion was "an object of silent struggles and silent opposition." Breuer reported that

> this girl, who was bubbling over with intellectual vitality, led an extremely monotonous existence in her puritanically-minded family. She embellished her life in a manner which probably influenced her decisively in the direction of her illness, by indulging in systematic daydreaming, which she described as her "private theater." While everyone thought she was attending, she was living through fairy tales in her imagination; but she was always on the spot when she was spoken to, so that no one was aware of it. She pursued this activity almost continuously while she was engaged on her household duties, which she discharged unexceptionably.

This was Bertha's life in the years before her hysterical breakdown. She had a split self, outwardly compliant and privately defiant. Her superior intelligence and imaginative gifts allowed her to live in two worlds at the same time, one the obedient Jewish wife-to-be and the other whatever she conjured up in the imaginative world of her "private theater."

The precipitating cause of her illness was her father's sickness and impending death. He contracted double pneumonia and, knowing that tuberculosis had killed two of their daughters, the family—and especially Bertha—were frightened that he too would die of the disease. Her hysterical symptoms made their first appearance as she sat by his bedside, nursing him through the night. She was about to lose the one family member whom she loved, and her ambivalent feelings were clamoring to be heard. Her divided self was breaking apart.

Breuer first attempted to treat her with hypnosis, urging her to recount the events related to her various symptoms, but found that "she was completely unsuggestable; she was only influenced by arguments, never by mere assertions." This attitude suited Breuer's personality, because he was uncomfortable in the role of controlling hypnotist, insisting that her symptoms go away. Together they worked out a unique approach, later called the cathartic method; in Bertha's own words it was "the talking cure" or, jokingly, "chimney sweeping." They were both more comfortable with this approach; it did not have the authoritarian quality that she was secretly in rebellion against. He came to see her every day and sometimes even twice a day. When her condition was at its worst, she could not leave her bed, so Breuer sat with her and encouraged her to talk, to tell a story or recount a fantasy. If she was unable to do so, he would listen to her "mutterings," repeat them to her, and help her get started. He also reverted to hypnosis from time to time and prescribed medications to alleviate her insomnia and physical pain; in short, he did all he could to relieve her distress.

This period lasted approximately a year and a half, during which he was able to connect many of Bertha's symptoms to specific events—usually frightening, distasteful, or traumatic events—that had occurred in the preceding months. He realized that the symptoms had meaning; they were symbols that expressed experiences Bertha could not put into words. A frequently cited incident was her inability to drink anything, even when the weather was extremely hot. She would start to drink from a glass of water and then push it away with fear. After about six weeks of this, Breuer heard her grumble about her English lady-companion, whom she did not like. She had seen "her little dog—'horrid creature!'—drink out of a glass.

The patient had said nothing, as she had wanted to be polite. After giving further energetic expression to the anger she had held back, she asked for something to drink, drank a large quantity of water. . . . Thereupon the disturbance vanished, never to return." The conflict here, like so many others, was between her anger and the "politeness" that kept her from expressing it openly.

Another example of symptoms closer to the center of her disturbance occurred as she sat by the bedside of her dying father:

> Her right arm [was] over the back of her chair. She fell into a waking dream and saw a black snake coming towards the sick man from the wall to bite him. . . . She tried to keep the snake off, but it was as though she was paralyzed. Her right arm, over the back of the chair, had gone to sleep and had become anaesthetic and paretic; and when she looked at it the fingers turned into little snakes with death's heads. . . . When the snake vanished, in her terror, she tried to pray. But language failed her: she could find no tongue in which to speak, till at last she thought of some children's verses in English and then found herself able to think and pray in that language.

The paralysis of her arm and her inability to speak or understand any language other than English first occurred in this context of fear and death. The symptoms then took on a life of their own, spreading out to related motor and language disturbances, though Bertha herself was not conscious of any of this and did not associate her symptoms with her original terror and death imagery.

Through his work with Bertha, Breuer developed two concepts that became staples of psychoanalysis: the unconscious mind and the symbolic expression of psychological conflicts. Another example further illustrates the link between symptoms and the unconscious. One evening Bertha sat by her dying father's bedside with tears in her eyes, and he asked her what time it was. She could not see clearly because of her tears, so she brought the watch close to her eyes, making the face seem very large. At the same time she was struggling to suppress her crying so that her father would not see it. From this incident emerged her "convergent squint" and related visual difficulties.

Disturbances in speech and communication were prominent throughout Bertha's illness. Breuer reported that

> for two weeks she became completely dumb and in spite of making great and continuous efforts to speak she was unable to say a syllable. And now for the first time the psychical mechanism for the disorder became clear. As I knew, she had felt very much offended over something and had determined not to speak about it. When I guessed this and obliged her to talk about it, the inhibition, which had made any other kind of utterance impossible as well, disappeared.

For years no one in Bertha's family understood her or knew what she was feeling or thinking. Any attempt to communicate with them must have seemed pointless to her. They did not want to know the real Bertha, so during her breakdown she "refused" to speak, or would only use a foreign language. In other words, her family's treatment of her was too painful for her to be consciously aware of, so her feelings about it could only emerge in emotional or symptomatic communications or lack of communication. By helping her put her affectively charged experiences into words, Breuer reversed the process, making conscious what had up to that point been kept out of awareness. This was the essence of his new cathartic method. Over the course of their intensive work, Breuer and Bertha traced a great number of her symptoms back to their origins. They recovered unconscious memories, put the experiences into words along with the stifled emotions, and alleviated her distress.

The process was not a smooth one. There were a number of relapses, but over time Bertha improved. Breuer's conclusion, stated in the article "Preliminary Communication," which also appears as the first chapter of *Studies*, was that

> each individual hysterical symptom immediately and permanently disappeared when we had succeeded in bringing clearly to light the

memory of the event by which it was provoked and in arousing its accompanying affect, and when the patient had described that event in the greatest possible detail and had put the affect into words.

In a famous summary statement, Breuer and Freud wrote, "Hysterics suffer mainly from reminiscences."

Throughout both "Preliminary Communication" and the case of Anna O., Breuer stressed the role of trauma. He was aware of earlier work that demonstrated the relationship between specific traumatic experiences, such as being in a train wreck, and the appearance of hysterical symptoms: "railway spine" and "railway brain." Similar symptoms were later seen in soldiers who survived the trench warfare of the First World War. Like the soldiers, Bertha and other women of her time were helplessly trapped in impossible positions. If the soldiers expressed their fear openly, they were branded as cowards or traitors; if the women complained about their suppression, they were branded as unfeminine, as striving to be men. The similar conflicts of both groups could only be expressed in a language of emotion and the body: trembling, nightmares, blindness, deafness, and paralysis—"hysteria."

The information presented in Anna O.'s case allows us to further our understanding of Bertha, using ideas that were not available in 1895. In addition to his emphasis on trauma, Breuer stressed the need for affective or emotional expression. This was crucial to his cathartic method, although Freud later moved in a different direction. It seems clear from Breuer's case report that along with emotional expression, his relationship with Bertha was a central part of her improvement, no doubt facilitated by his kind, empathic personality and the great amount of time he devoted to her care. Breuer was the only person she would talk to most of the time; she reassured herself that it was him by feeling his hands. When she refused to eat, he fed her, and her condition became worse when he left on vacation, only to improve when he returned. The strength of the doctor-patient rapport is undeniable. Although Breuer reported all these occurrences, he did not comment on their importance to her recovery. As a physician he saw his patient through a medical lens; his paramount concern was to alleviate her symptoms. He encouraged her to give verbal and affective expression to her memories, believing that this would effect a cure.

Another aspect of the psychology of the case that Breuer did not comment on was her mixed feelings toward her father. Although he described her split personality in some detail, and even related it to the sterile and empty life that was forced upon her, he did not take his observations further and relate them to the love-hate relationship that she most certainly had with her father. Ambivalence is a word that hardly does justice to Bertha's overwhelming conflict. We know today that patients like her have almost always suffered severe conflicts and traumas. In Bertha's case, she was "passionately" attached to her father; he was all she had in the family. At the same time, it was he who imprisoned her in the role of Orthodox Jewish woman, and her anger at him—perhaps even the wish that he die—was powerfully threatening. At that time in her life she could only experience her conflicting emotions as death-dealing black snakes—hallucinations that arose in her mind—which frightened her terribly. Her anger at her father was far too threatening for her to be aware of it, especially as he lay dying. It could only exist in what she called her "evil self"; it could not be expressed in words by the "real her."

Bertha was emotionally isolated in her family. Her mother and brother seemed largely unaware of her inner life, her most significant hopes, longings, and dissatisfactions. Several months into her illness, as she nursed her father, no one even noticed her symptoms or moods. When she was at the height of her disturbance, and her father was dying, her family prevented her from seeing him. Bertha experienced this as an unforgivable betrayal, a neglect of her deepest feelings, as intolerable "lies." This was a rare instance of open anger at her family members, though she had good reason for these feelings, including the preferential treatment her brother received. Throughout her earlier years she went about her duties with an entirely separate, secret self, and no one seemed to notice.

What is one to make of her "passionate" attachment to her father, a love that precluded relationships with other men? Martha Freud commented that the attractive Bertha had the power "to turn the head of the most sensible of men." Yet as far as is known, she never had any intimate male relationships. Loving a man might have meant complying with the family's requirement that she become a good, Orthodox Jewish wife, something she secretly fought against. Another possibility is that her father wanted her tied to him (as Freud did years later with his daughter Anna) and interfered with other potential relationships. Her later writings are dominated by the theme of unhappy girls who have been abandoned and mistreated, and eventually, in her life's work, she was devoted to saving girls and young women who were the victims of male cruelty.

To sum up Breuer's accomplishments in his treatment of Bertha Pappenheim, above all he had a clear understanding that hysteria is a psychological condition and not due to such things as "neurological degeneration," "hereditary predisposition" (Charcot's theory) or "over-excitement of the nervous system," as others had speculated. He also understood that her many symptoms and mental states had meaning, that they were the way she symbolically communicated her fear, anger, and dissatisfaction. He realized that, to be effective, the therapy must be accompanied by full affective or emotional expression. Breuer was aware of the significance of sexual conflicts in hysteria, as his other writings show, and he was surprised by their absence in Bertha. In "Preliminary Communication" he focused on the central role of trauma and the variety of emotions involved, such as fright, anger, shame, disgust, sadness, revenge, and guilt. He did not attempt to reduce his understanding of hysteria to any one emotional conflict, and he recognized that sexual feeling was one state among many. In addition, his work with his patient was a collaboration; the "talking cure" and "chimney sweeping" were Bertha's terms, and it is obvious throughout his case report that, far from imposing his authority, he continuously modified his approach in response to her reactions. He tried to free his patient of her painful symptoms by encouraging her to tell stories, relate her fantasies, and in other ways put her physical and emotional experiences into words, to communicate them to an interested and sympathetic listener. Although he did not say as much, he provided her with the relationship that had been missing in her life before she began seeing him.

There has been a good deal of controversy about the end of Breuer's work with Bertha. In *Studies* he concludes, "She was moreover free from the innumerable disturbances which she had previously exhibited. After this she left Vienna and traveled for a while; but it was a considerable time before she regained her mental balance entirely. Since then she has enjoyed complete health."

We now know that it took over six years for Bertha to recover fully and that Breuer was involved in her treatment during that period. In the earlier phase of her cathartic therapy, he would sometimes prescribe the common sleeping medication chloral hydrate to help with her insomnia, and she eventually became addicted to it, as she did to morphine, which he prescribed for her facial pain. He eventually placed her in Robert Binswanger's Kreuzlingen Sanatorium in Switzerland, one of the most advanced treatment centers in the world, to wean her from her addictions. His long report about Bertha—composed in 1882 or 1883, and unearthed by his biographer, Albrecht Hirschmüller, many years later—forms the basis for the case report in *Studies*. It was written for Binswanger to help him understand and treat Bertha. Among other things, Breuer wrote to her new doctor, "I hope that my patient, who has always meant a great deal to me, will soon be safely in your care."

Bertha's mother, with whom she had been on bad terms, eventually became involved in her life. They reconciled and, with the help of a large and supportive group of relatives—one of whom encouraged her to pursue her literary interests—she gradually recovered from the worst features of her mental illness. The imaginative gifts that Breuer noted in *Studies* led Bertha to write a series of fairy tales, children's stories, and poems, all of which were infused with the themes of thwarted love, children in need of care, and the exploitation of girls and women by men. A mood of unrelieved melancholy pervades almost all her tales. Although Breuer's statement that it took a "considerable time" until she regained her mental balance is not incorrect, he failed to mention the addictions and the time she spent in sanitaria, perhaps for reasons of confidentiality. In later life Bertha never referred to her breakdown and treatment by Breuer; in fact, she destroyed all her papers and letters from the years before 1890.

Freud's "reconstruction" of the story of Anna O. is the ugly aftermath to Breuer's work and is key to understanding the way he dealt with many of his later psychoanalytic colleagues when they did not completely agree with him. Of the *Five Lectures* that he delivered at Clark University in 1909, the first is devoted to Breuer's case. He gives his former collaborator credit for the invention of psychoanalysis, and the treatment of Anna/Bertha is described in much the same way as it appears in *Studies*. However, in his 1914 *On the History of the Psycho-analytic Movement*, he backs away from this position, minimizes Breuer's contribution, and gives greater emphasis to his own discoveries. Freud states, "I have come to the conclusion that I must be the true originator of all that is particularly characteristic in [psychoanalysis]." He continues with a reinterpretation of Bertha's symptoms in sexual terms—the snakes and her stiff limbs are phallic symbols—and speculates that she had an erotic transference to her physician. He continues,

> Now I have strong reasons for suspecting that after all her symptoms had been relieved Breuer must have discovered from further indications the sexual motivation of this transference, but that the universal nature of this unexpected phenomenon escaped him, with the result that, as though confronted by an "untoward event" he broke off all further investigation. He never said this to me in so many words, but he told me enough at different times to justify this reconstruction of what happened.

Freud repeats this story in his 1925 *Autobiographical Study*, reporting that Breuer "retired in dismay" when confronted with Bertha's "transference love." Finally, in a letter to the writer Stefan Zweig, Freud embellished the tale by adding that the erotic transference manifested itself in a hysterical birth fantasy and that Breuer was called to the Pappenheim home to find Bertha saying she was about to "give birth to Dr. Breuer's baby." This letter was written in 1932, fifty years after Breuer treated Bertha and thirty-seven years after the publication of *Studies*. Ernest Jones accepted Freud's tale and even embellished it in his 1953 biography. In his version, not only did Breuer break off all treatment when the sexual transference appeared, but his wife was jealous and, feeling guilty, he took her on a second honey-moon to Venice, where their daughter Dora was conceived. Years later Dora committed suicide, in Jones's version giving some sort of fitting end to Breuer's failure to deal with Bertha's sexual transference.

Freud's distorted version of the case, and Jones's further elaboration of it, attempt to portray Breuer as a coward and Freud as a hero. These stories emphasize that the older, more experienced doctor presumably did not have the courage to face up to his patient's sexuality, whereas Freud not only did so with his patients, but placed sexuality at the center of his theory of neurosis. This account of the conclusion of Bertha's treatment has passed into psychoanalytic lore and been endlessly recycled by a number of the faithful.

But Freud's version of what happened is simply not true. It is an example of the "resistance" argument that he later used to dismiss everyone who raised questions about his theory of sexuality: They could not accept it because it was too personally threatening. The truth is that Breuer did not flee from Bertha but remained involved with her treatment for several years. He and his wife did not vacation in Venice that year; his daughter Dora was born in March 1882, three months before the end of his cathartic treatment of Bertha; and she did not commit suicide in New York, but rather stayed in Vienna after 1938 to help her sister's family. She died at the hands of the Nazis in 1942.

There is a germ of truth in Freud's story. Breuer continued to see other women suffering from hysteria, though he no longer employed the cathartic method. The older physician did not pursue the discoveries he had made with Bertha Pappenheim; although he continued to see psychiatric patients, he did not use the cathartic technique he first invented with her. The reasons for this are probably far different from those espoused by Freud and Jones. In a letter about his work with Bertha Pappenheim, written to the Swiss psychiatrist Auguste Forel in 1907, Breuer said, "this immersion in the sexual in theory and practice is not to my taste." Breuer and Bertha no doubt were very attached to one another; she was an attractive young woman, and this may have made him uncomfortable at times. His wife could easily have become resentful of the great amount of attention that he gave to his female patient. But this does not support Freud's claim that Breuer was frightened off by sexuality, because in fact, he did not flee from his work with Bertha. What is more, he was aware, from his earlier familiarity with hypnotic demonstrations, that women were known to kiss or embrace their hypnotists, so if signs of his patient's attraction appeared, he would not have been surprised. I think we must take him at his word when he says that no sexuality appeared in her many communications, fantasies, or hallucinations. If any one emotional state was prominent, it was her tremendous conflict over the anger she experienced and the prohibitions, both internal and external, that made its expression impossible.

Breuer also wrote to Forel,

> The main contribution that can be credited to me is that I recognized what an enormously instructive, scientifically important case chance had assigned to me for treatment, and that I persevered in attentive and faithful observation and did not disturb the simple apprehension of the important facts with preconceived notions. In this way I learned many things, things valuable from a scientific view, but also . . . that it is impossible for a general practitioner to treat such a case without having his practice and private life completely ruined by it. At the time, I swore never again to submit to such an ordeal. So when cases came to me . . . which I could not treat myself, I referred them to Dr. Freud.

Reading the case, it is clear that after all the time Breuer gave to Bertha, and the success that was achieved with the cathartic method, he had to deal with her addiction to drugs he had prescribed and periodic relapses. Those who have worked with very disturbed patients such as these are aware that such therapy is extremely difficult; it is both time consuming and emotionally draining. Patients like Bertha display a number of highly disruptive emotions: powerful anxiety, depression that can reach suicidal extremes, fragmentation of the self, and loss of the sense of reality. Even with our present-day understanding, traumatized patients with multiple self-states are very difficult to work with, and Breuer did not have the benefit of our

current knowledge. Given that he was a busy physician and scientific inves-
tigator, it is not surprising that he decided "never again [to] submit to
such an ordeal." He passed such patients on to his younger colleague, who
was still struggling to establish his practice and only too happy to accept
them.

    This account fits with the picture of Bertha that emerges from the case
report and is consistent with her later life history. It also fits with what we
know today about patients such as these, that trauma is much more prevalent than sexual conflicts, and is confirmed by the pattern of Freud's later
attacks on many other collaborators—Adler, Jung, Stekel, Rank, and Ferenczi—when they dared to question his theory of sexuality. In addition,
unlike Breuer, Freud would not have credited Bertha's oppression as a
woman as a cause of her condition, because he believed that assuming a
subservient role was woman's natural place. During his courtship of
Martha he rejected John Stuart Mill's ideas about the rights of women,
and after their marriage he treated his wife in much the same way that
Bertha's father had treated her. In his view, women should stay at home
and be content with their roles as dutiful wives and mothers. As he later
speculated, babies would provide a substitute for the penises they lacked.

In 1888, when the worst of Bertha's psychological distress had passed, she
and her mother moved to Frankfurt, Germany, where the mother had a
large number of wealthy Jewish relatives who were cultured and involved in
charitable activities. At the urging of a cousin, Bertha initially devoted herself to writing. This literary work had been foreshadowed by the stories
and fantasies she told Breuer during her cathartic treatment and by the
fairy tales she wrote shortly before her move to Frankfurt. At first she published children's stories, but over time her writing became more political
and polemical. She even wrote a play, *A Woman's Right*, about a husband's exploitation of his wife who, in the end, exerts her "woman's right" by refus-
ing to have sex with him. In 1899 she published the first German

translation of Mary Wollstonecraft's *A Vindication of the Rights of Women*, including a preface in which she declared that women's struggle for equality was as necessary at the end of the nineteenth century as it was when Wollstonecraft wrote at the end of the eighteenth. Bertha also discovered a distant ancestor of hers, Gluckel von Hameln, who in the late seventeenth to early eighteenth centuries had become educated and achieved equality with her husband. Inspired by this predecessor, Bertha translated von Hameln's memoirs and even had her own portrait painted, dressed as Gluckel, and titled it, "Bertha Pappenheim as Gluckel." With these and other feminist models, she constructed a new identity from the fragments of her old self.

Around the turn of the century Bertha became involved in social work, further linking her own experience with those of other young women who had struggled with overwhelming difficulties. In 1894 she joined the Jewish Woman's Union, an organization dedicated to bringing up orphan girls, at first as a volunteer. In 1897, following the death of the matron, Bertha became her successor. In addition to holding this position, she was involved with schools and girls' clubs, organizations devoted to helping orphans, and the League of Jewish Women, which she began in 1904 and served as president for many years. With her own money and outside contributions, she established a home for abandoned and abused girls that she ran for many years. In her work with all these organizations, she was concerned with providing aid to unmarried mothers and their children, caring for the homeless, helping women abandoned by their husbands, offering vocational training, and treating those afflicted with tuberculosis, the disease that had killed her father. Of particular importance was her devotion to the abolition of white slavery (back in the news today as "trafficking"), the procurement of poor Jewish girls from Eastern Europe for prostitution. She unofficially adopted several poor girls and sponsored their training and education. She eventually became known as the first social worker in Germany, and a postage stamp was issued by the government in her honor in 1945, one of a series titled "Helpers of Humanity."

Bertha's personality in these years was an amalgam of contradictory characteristics; a colleague described "the unique harmony of severity and loving kindness, gravity and gaiety, cultivated femininity and amazing strength of will." She took on projects that were very unusual for an upper-class woman of her time. Charitable work typically meant simply giving money, with only occasional volunteer activities, but Bertha threw herself into this work full time and was a fierce champion of her causes. She was severe and fiery in her protests against inequality and fought, with an iron will, against those who disagreed with her. Her coworkers spoke of "a live volcano within her." She was strong and domineering in pursuit of her goals and had a dark and pessimistic attitude. In other ways, she returned to the values and ideas of her youth, resolving her earlier conflicts about religion, and once again became committed to Judaism. The harsh and unforgiving conscience that was one feature of her hysteria was now turned on those who opposed her goals. But she was gentle, kind, and loving with the children in her care: When the staff at the children's home had arranged a birthday celebration for her, she became so choked up with emotion that she said, through her tears, "Forgive me, I am so little used to affection that you have quite overwhelmed me." Her contrasting qualities are the remnants of the two selves of her earlier life. She still had somewhat of a split personality, but clearly the division did not cause her the anguish it had during the years of her breakdown.

Throughout her later years Bertha said many times that love had passed her by, that she felt isolated and preferred to focus on the beautiful objects she collected or commissioned from craftsmen. She enjoyed good food and resumed playing the piano. A poem she composed in 1911 captures a central feeling about her life:

> *Love did not come to me—*
> *So I live like the plants,*
> *In the cellar, without light.*

> *Love did not come to me—*
> *So I sound like a violin*
> *With a broken bow.*

Love did not come to me—
So I bury myself in work
And, chastened, live for duty.

Love did not come to me—
So I like to think of death
As a friendly face.

Outside of her work with children and young women, many of whom felt great affection for her, "love did not come to her." So far as is known, Bertha never had intimate sexual relations with anyone, and devoted a great portion of her life to combating the unscrupulous sexual exploitation of women by men. And this brings us back to ways of understanding her breakdown and recovery. The simplest explanation is that she was caught in a terrible conflict between her innate energy and talent and the stifling role forced on her as an Orthodox Jewish woman. Breuer entertained this explanation, but wondered whether it was sufficient to account for the degree and intensity of her disturbance. No doubt her fiery, volcanic temperament caused the conflict to be more powerful for her than it would have been for a milder, more malleable person like Martha Bernays Freud. Bertha also possessed an unrelenting, punitive conscience, both during her breakdown—as seen in her inability to express her anger or frustration directly in words—and, in later life, in the severe standards to which she held herself and that she attempted to force on everyone who interfered with her altruistic goals. She was a woman of conviction who wouldn't compromise her principles.

Another factor in her breakdown was the loss and deprivation she experienced growing up. Her mother was unavailable to her, and the impending loss of her father was the precipitating cause of her illness. Despite her evident attractiveness to men—as mentioned by her friend, Martha Freud—she was not interested in romance. In her early twenties she rejected the consolations of music and pretty things, which she associated with the trivial and meaningless life that was being forced on her. The care she lavished on poor and abandoned girls was a vicarious enjoyment of what was missing in her own life. Although she was eventually able to put her brilliance and energy to use and to achieve a great deal in her lifetime, in the end she remained sad and unloved.

We are left with the question of what role Breuer's treatment played in Bertha's recovery. Many of the qualities that he described—her marked intelligence, penetrating intuition, poetic and imaginative gifts, tenacious and persistent willpower and, of special importance, the relief she experienced when she was able to help poor, sick people or rescue animals from danger—came to fruition in later life. It seems likely that Breuer's cathartic treatment played an important role in her recovery and eventual ability to apply her gifts to meaningful work, that he helped release her from her frightened and conflicted symptomatic state. But we will never know for certain because she never said anything about the earlier period of her life. Perhaps the reason she never spoke about it later was that the breakdown was too painful. Anyone who has experienced the years of horrific distress, terror, and conflict that constituted her "hysterical" illness is determined never to feel such things again, never to revisit that period. Breuer also vowed "never again [to] submit to such an ordeal." Bertha needed the severe discipline and emotional control that characterized her later life to protect her sanity. Intimate relationships were not an option. The satisfactions of her writing, translations, aesthetic objects, and work with abused girls and women were her consolations. She was the first psychoanalytic case, but this was not as significant for her as the fulfillment she obtained through her committed service to women.

CHAPTER FIVE

Meaning Out of Chaos

Much illness is a conflict in values sailing under a physiological flag.

RUDOLF VIRCHOW
German physician/scientist, 1821–1902

*T*he case histories Freud presented in *Studies on Hysteria*, along with Breuer's account of Bertha Pappenheim and a scattering of other vignettes, are the foundation on which all of psychoanalysis is based. It is vital to look in detail at this material to see who these women were, what made up their "hysteria," and how they were treated.

Freud was still working closely with Breuer in 1887 when, encouraged by his mentor, he began to see his own patients, using the cathartic method. The woman he treated the longest during this period appears only briefly in *Studies*, probably for reasons of confidentiality. He referred to her as "Cäcilie M.," but she was really the Baroness Anna von Lieben. She was over forty years old when she began her treatment, and he saw her every day in her home, sometimes more than once a day. At first he hypnotized her and told her that, when she was brought out of her trance, her symptoms would be gone. She also traveled with him to Nancy, where he went to perfect his technique with the French hypnotism experts Ambroise Liébeault and Hippolyte Bernheim. But hypnotic suggestion seemed to produce only temporary relief of von Lieben's suffering, and he moved on to a method that, to some extent, presaged his later version of psychoanalysis.

Freud referred to von Lieben as his "teacher" and "prima donna" because, through working together, they were able to confirm the psychological meaning of many of her symptoms. As he put it, "The only way of relieving her was to give her an opportunity of talking off under hypnosis the particular reminiscence which was tormenting her at the moment, together with all its accompanying load of feelings and their physical expression." He worked with her for over three years and managed to process more than thirty years' worth of what he termed "old debts": traumatic memories extending back into her childhood.

Anna Von Lieben was born into an extremely wealthy family, married a rich banker, had five children, and lived a life of luxury in their palace in Vienna and summer villa. Eccentric and domineering, she became quite obese over the years, a condition she treated for a time with a diet of caviar and champagne. She was skilled at chess, could play two games at the same time, and sometimes kept a professional player outside her bedroom all night in case she woke and felt like having a game. She alternately took her children into her bed or ignored them completely. About five years before she first saw Freud, she became addicted to morphine, which she took to relieve her symptoms. It is impossible to judge how much of her unstable emotional state was due to the use of and withdrawal from morphine and how much to her "hysteria."

Despite her life of indolence and privilege, von Lieben suffered from a number of severe symptoms and spent a great deal of her life in bed, attended by doctors who attempted to provide some relief. The failure of these treatments led her to consult Freud and to try the new cathartic approach. She was quite intelligent and, like Bertha Pappenheim, possessed literary gifts; she wrote and published a number of poems starting in adolescence. She had suffered from her symptoms since she was fifteen, and although Freud's treatment provided some relief, they soon returned, and remained with her for the rest of her life.

Breuer was the von Lieben family physician and recommended Freud as someone who might alleviate her facial pains, inexplicable mood swings, hallucinations, muscle spasms, and feelings of worthlessness. Freud felt he had learned so much in his work with this "teacher" that he urged a reluctant Breuer to join him in publishing their work, first in the journal article "Preliminary Communication" in 1893 and, two years later, in *Studies on Hysteria*.

Most striking to both Freud and Breuer were the symbolic connections that were made between particular symptoms and past traumatic events. In one session von Lieben described a fight with her husband in which she interpreted a remark of his as "a bitter insult." As Freud put it, "Suddenly, she put her hand to her cheek, gave a loud cry of pain, and said: 'it was like a slap in the face.' With this her pain and her attack were both at an end." On another occasion she felt "a violent pain in her right heel" which appeared when she was frightened that she might not "find herself on the right footing" with a group of strangers. She also recounted a vivid experience when her illness first appeared in her teens. One day her strict grandmother gave her a critical look that she described as extremely "piercing." The threatening glare resulted in a penetrating pain in the young girl's forehead. In each of these examples, when Freud was able to uncover the old memory, and von Lieben could put it into words with its accompanying emotion, she obtained relief.

These symbolic connections made clear to both Freud and his patient the psychological meaning of her symptoms; they even had a poetic flare that made them quite persuasive to him. But this kind of metaphoric expression is not commonly found in the body language of people experiencing unconscious conflicts. Bertha Pappenheim's symptoms, for the most part, were of a more general nature—terrors, paralyses, sleep disturbance—which is more typical of what one sees in such cases. Freud acknowledged as much in *Studies* when, in writing about von Lieben, he noted, "I have not found such an extensive use of symbolization in any other patient." Nevertheless, given his own literary proclivities, this kind of symbolism had an appeal to him and influenced his later modification of the cathartic approach, in which he deemphasized the importance of emotional release and stressed this sort of interpretive decoding.

Freud was much taken with von Lieben, but he was not able to present her case in detail, so there is no information that would allow a more complete understanding of her severe disturbance. From the few examples that

Freud does provide, the conflicts behind her symptoms were similar to those of Bertha Pappenheim. She was insulted (the "slap in the face") but did not allow herself to respond; people mistreated her and she had to "swallow it" (stifle her anger), which led to problems with her mouth and throat; her grandmother was critical, which caused a stabbing pain in her head. All of these symptoms involved what Breuer and Freud would term the "strangulated affect" of anger in response to hurtful acts. As in the case of Bertha, no sexual conflicts were mentioned. Freud's treatment of von Lieben was of temporary help, but she did not make a lasting recovery. She died of a heart condition at age fifty-three.

Although Anna von Lieben was the first case that Freud treated with the cathartic method, there are only scattered mentions of her in *Studies*. Breuer never saw any more cases using the cathartic method after Bertha Pappenheim, though he and his younger colleague continued, for a few years, to discuss the patients Freud treated. When they came to publish *Studies*, all the long case reports, other than Anna O.'s, were Freud's. Four patients are described in detail.

The first full case that Freud presented was the Baroness Fanny Moser, given the pseudonym "Emmy von N." She was a forty-year-old widow with two adolescent daughters when she first came to see him in 1888, when he was still treating von Lieben. He was quite impressed with Frau Moser and spoke of her "unusual degree of education and intelligence, [how she] still looked young and had finely-cut features, full of character, [and how her] symptoms and personality interested me so greatly that I devoted a large part of my time to her and determined to do all I could for her recovery."

Frau Moser, like Bertha Pappenheim and Anna von Lieben, suffered a plethora of symptoms. Her speech was distorted, she displayed "tic-like movements of her face," and she would emit a "curious clacking sound." Although she was able to provide Freud with a coherent account of her troubles, from time to time she would extend her hands toward him, as if warding him off, and say, with great fear, "Keep still! Don't say anything!

Don't touch me!" She would then resume talking as if unaware of her outburst. Freud said, "She was probably under the influence of some recurrent hallucination of a horrifying kind and was keeping the intruding material at bay with this formula." In addition, she was depressed, had insomnia, was "tormented" by pains in different parts of her body, was phobic about animals, had difficulties eating, and was afraid she would be put in an insane asylum and mistreated. Her high level of anxiety caused her to become startled at any unexpected movement, such as someone opening a door or touching her. She dated the onset of her illness to the time of her husband's death, fourteen years earlier, a severe trauma that resonated with the many deaths of her early years.

Frau Moser was the thirteenth of fourteen children. She was born into a propertied family that was stalked by death. Four of her siblings died as infants, before she was born. Two died in infancy when she was very young and another when she was around age four. A sister died when Frau Moser was eighteen, and a brother, who was addicted to morphine, died when she was twenty. Only four of her thirteen brothers and sisters survived. When she was fifteen years old, she came home one day to find her mother lying unconscious on the floor, having suffered a stroke. She recovered, but four years later her young daughter found her dead in the house. Frau Moser reported a number of other terrifying memories to Freud: "When I was five years old . . . my brother and sister often threw dead animals at me. . . . I was frightened again when I was seven and unexpectedly saw my sister in a coffin . . . and again when I was nine and I saw my aunt in her coffin and her jaw suddenly dropped."

In addition to enduring an overwhelming number of deaths, Frau Moser, like Bertha Pappenheim, suffered from a punitive conscience. Freud reflected on her "moral seriousness," which he thought was a virtue, but also noted the extent of her "self-reproaches," and her "morally over-sensitive personality with its tendency to self-depreciation." As he commented, "She was brought up carefully, but under strict discipline by an over-energetic and severe mother."

The great trauma of her adult life was the death of her husband and the troubles that followed from it. At age twenty-three she married Heinrich Moser, an extremely wealthy industrialist forty years her senior, and they had two daughters. A few days after the birth of their second child, she was lying in bed with her husband sitting nearby when he fell to the floor, dead of a heart attack.

As she told Freud during her treatment,

> The baby had been seized with a serious illness which had lasted for six months, during which she herself had been in bed with a high fever. . . . There now followed . . . her grievances against this child, which she threw out rapidly with an angry look on her face. . . . She said, she had hated her child for three years, because she always told herself she might have been able to nurse her husband back to health if she had not been in bed on account of the child.

As if the sudden death of her husband were not calamity enough—and one that echoed the many deaths she experienced as a child—"His relatives, who had always been against the marriage and had been angry because they had been so happy together, had spread a rumour that she had poisoned him." An autopsy revealed that this was not true. Her husband had left a large part of his enormous fortune to Fanny and their daughters, making her one of the richest women in Europe. Many of the attacks on her came from the older children of his first marriage and were motivated by their desire to get their hands on this inheritance, along with jealousy of their father's young wife. The rumors and attacks continued for many years and, as Fanny said, her fear and distrust of people came from the persecution she suffered after her husband's death.

At the outset of the treatment, Freud told Frau Moser to put her two daughters, now in their teens, in the hands of their governess and enter a nursing home, where he saw her every day. She was very easy to hypnotize, and when she entered this state, he would instruct her to report the associations of her many fears and symptoms. His treatment combined the recovery and expression of frightening and traumatic memories (catharsis) with hypnotic suggestions that she banish all these memories and emotions from her mind. As he put it when he later wrote up her case in *Studies*, "My therapy consists in wiping away these pictures, so that she is no longer able to see them before her." With Frau Moser he played the role of doctor-authority, ordering his patient to banish disturbing material from her thoughts. This was one of his first cases, and he was eager to cure her. He would "wipe away" her fears and pains, both by telling her she would not remember them and by literally wiping his hand across her face. On one occasion, when she complained of stomach pains, he instructed her that they would be gone when she awoke and stroked her stomach. He used massage with her, which helped her relax and alleviated some of her anxiety. Despite his authoritative use of posthypnotic suggestion, he also listened sympathetically to everything she reported, attempted to calm her, confirmed her accounts, and assured her that she would get better.

Although Freud was able to "expunge" many of Frau Moser's fears and memories during his sessions with her, there were still a few occasions when she recovered memories outside of a hypnotic state. In *Studies* Freud noted that she "said in a definitely grumbling tone that I was not to keep on asking her where this or that came from, but let her tell me what she had to say. I fell in with this." She described her feelings at the time her husband's body was carried out and her difficulty believing he was really dead. At another point Freud said that there were "pathogenic reminiscences of which [Frau Moser] unburdens herself without being asked to. It is as though she had adopted my procedure and was making use of our conversation, apparently unconstrained and guided by chance, as a supplement to her hypnosis."

In Freud's summary of the origin of Frau Moser's condition, he made the connections between symptoms and life events which, although perhaps obvious to us now, were new discoveries at the time:

> Specific phobias were also accounted for by particular events. Her dread of unexpected and sudden shocks was the consequence of the terrible impression made on her by seeing her husband, when he seemed to be in the best of health, succumb to a heart attack before her eyes. Her dread of strangers, and of people in general, turned out to be derived from the time when she was being persecuted by her husband's family and was inclined to see one of their agents in every

stranger and when it seemed to her likely that strangers knew of the things that were being spread abroad about her in writing and by word of mouth. [Being so wealthy made her a celebrity and the target of gossip of the kind still prevalent today.] Her fear of asylums and their inmates went back to a whole series of unhappy events in her family [involving her mother's and other relatives' confinement to mental institutions]. Her old-established disgust at meal times had persisted undiminished because she was obliged constantly to suppress it, instead of getting rid of it by reaction. In her childhood she had been forced, under threat of punishment, to eat the cold meal that disgusted her.

Freud came to realize that her other symptoms—the facial tics, the "clacking sound," her "Keep still!" injunction, and the rest—were similarly connected to specific events in her life. For example, the "Don't touch me!" command had its origin in a memory from age nineteen when her morphine-addicted brother would seize hold of her in a frightening and painful way. In all these examples Freud, like Breuer before him, connected his patient's symptoms to actual traumatic events; there was no speculation about sexual drives or fantasies as causes, with one exception. Toward the end of his summary, Freud guessed that

> amongst all the intimate information given me by the patient there was a complete absence of the sexual element, which is, after all, more liable than any other to provide occasion for traumas. . . . I cannot help suspecting that this woman who was so passionate and so capable of strong feelings had not won her victory over her sexual needs without severe struggles, and that at times her attempts at suppressing this most powerful of all instincts had exposed her to severe mental exhaustion.

This was the first appearance of what would within a few years become the core of his new theory. Later in his case report he commented, "It is necessary, I think, to adduce a neurotic factor to account for this persist-ence [of her phobias]—the fact that the patient had been living for years in a state of sexual abstinence. Such circumstances are among the most frequent causes of a tendency to anxiety." When writing about her, he speculated about the role of sexuality because Frau Moser never talked about it. The truth was that she was very sexually active during and after the years Freud saw her. As she herself told him, "She had not married again because, in view of her large fortune, she could not credit the disinterestedness of her suitors and because she would have reproached herself for damaging the prospects of her two children by a new marriage." She worked out a compromise in which she took a series of lovers, often the personal physicians who lived in her house, and attempted to be discreet about these affairs. But those who knew her spoke of her "erotic extravagance." In the case of Bertha Pappenheim, Breuer took the absence of sexuality at face value and constructed his explanation from the evidence before him. Frau Moser's traumas were even more blatant, so one wonders why Freud needed to speculate about her sexuality or any other factors. Could all the deaths she experienced have reverberated uncomfortably with the losses he had experienced in his own childhood? Did he need to escape from these threatening feelings by speculating about the role of sexual abstinence that, as it turned out, never existed?

Freud saw Frau Moser for a short time in 1888 and believed, with her compliant agreement, that he had cured most of her symptoms. As he put it, "My patient's condition improved so rapidly, that she soon assured me she had not felt so well since her husband's death. After a treatment lasting in all seven weeks I allowed her to return to her home." Yet Breuer had taken over a year and a half to help Bertha Pappenheim, and it took several more years for her to make a full recovery. Freud's own work with Anna von Lieben had gone on for over three years, at the end of which she was still symptomatic. Indeed, one feels that Freud's need to produce a rapid cure to prove his mettle as a doctor took precedence over his patient's welfare.

Sure enough, one year later Frau Moser returned, again unwell. Freud's view was that "by an act of will as it were, she undid the effects of my treatment and promptly relapsed into the states from which I had freed her." She did not display the same symptoms as she had the previous year, but was now complaining of "storms in her head [and] . . . sleeplessness, and was often in tears for hours at a time. . . . She stammered and clacked a great deal and kept rubbing her hands together as though she was in a rage, and when I asked her if she saw a great many animals, she only replied: 'Oh keep still!'"

In this second round of treatment, which lasted eight weeks, Freud again used hypnotic suggestion to wipe away her symptoms. If he was at all tentative in his role as authoritative doctor in 1888, one year later he was more confident. At one point he initiated a power struggle, deciding to "feed her up a little"—a throwback to the Weir Mitchell method with its use of a special diet—insisting that it was her fear rather than her "constitution" that made it impossible for her to eat and drink. He seemed to have forgotten that being forced to eat had been a major conflict with her mother, and he threatened to break off the treatment if she did not follow his prescription. After he successfully pressured her in this way, she finally became "docile and submissive," and when he asked her about her gastric pains, she replied, "I think they come from my anxiety, but only because you say so." She had submitted to his authority. In addition to using hypnotic suggestion, he "fought against the patient's pathological ideas by means of assurances and prohibitions, and by putting forward opposing ideas of every sort."

When she was overcome with fear about her daughter's health, Freud attempted to combat it by pointing out that the girl was perfectly well. He did come to see, for the most part, that such measures were of little avail. What information he received about her in the next few years indicated that, although showing some improvement, she was by no means cured, a fact he was honest enough to admit. As he put it, "The therapeutic success on the whole was considerable; but it was not a lasting one."

His balanced concluding discussion of this case stressed the confirmation of Breuer's discovery of the psychological meaning of symptoms of which the patient is unconscious; the significance of trauma, with the one intrusion of his speculation about her sexual abstinence; and the importance of childhood antecedents. He recognized that, because he had combined catharsis with hypnotic suggestion, he could not know which was effective in the improvement Frau Moser achieved.

I would characterize her state when she returned to Freud as that of a trauma survivor who has had her highly disruptive memories partly opened up—her modes of adaptation interfered with—only to have them shut down again. The "storms in the head" may have been a way of expressing this confused emotional state, and the endless crying an outpouring of the grief over all the deaths and losses in her life that she had become aware of, only to have her doctor attempt to expunge them. Freud tracked down the meaning of almost every tic, fear, and pain, but never discussed her tears and upwelling sadness.

Like many severely traumatized people, Frau Moser's self was fragmented, split, "dissociated." She was outwardly compliant, both with her doctor and others in her life, where she was concerned to present a "morally serious," respectable façade, "no less than a man's," as Freud commented. But her many trauma-related emotions kept breaking through this surface: A voice that she does not experience as her own says, "Keep still!—Don't say anything!—Don't touch me!" During her second treatment, when Freud was once again trying to wipe away her memories, "it" told him, "Oh, keep still!" In Freud's discussion of her case, he describes the effects of the overwhelming traumas in her life and then moves away from them with his speculations about her sexual abstinence.

Although she easily relived her many traumatic experiences under hypnosis, often seeing them as if they were actually occurring before her eyes, when Frau Moser was brought out of her trance and prompted by his suggestions, she had no memory of these terrifying hallucinations. Nevertheless, they continued to exist in the split-off part of herself, pressing to be heard, known, recognized. Although her dissociated experiences received some recognition in the cathartic part of her treatment, Freud's commitment to "curing" her interfered with an understanding of her symptoms and an integration of her traumatic experiences into her conscious self. Her attempts to communicate via symptom and symbol were largely unheard, and her anger at that had to be suppressed. Freud then interpreted this as her keeping secrets from him, or as "an act of will" by which she

undid the cure he had achieved with her. She broke off her second treatment, telling him she was better, only to seek out a series of other doctors
in the following years.

Frau Moser's life after her treatment by Freud was an artistically and intellectually, not to mention erotically, stimulating one. Faced with continued persecution, she used her wealth to escape to a castle on a lake in
Switzerland, which she had bought the year before she first consulted
Freud. There she lived as "a salon hostess, an admired eccentric, a philan-
thropist and patron of arts, a woman of extravagant lifestyle and opinions,
much respected by the artists and scientists whom she entertained." She
was very generous in her support of talented individuals in need.

Frau Moser functioned reasonably well for some years, given her very
traumatic background and the extent of her psychological disturbance.
Her wealth no doubt helped, though it was a mixed blessing, because she
could never trust the motives of the men who were interested in her. In
later years she took a young lover, who plundered part of her fortune. She
died at the age of seventy-six, suffering from the delusion that she was destitute and could not even afford her next meal, even though she still had
millions. A sad end to the life of this highly intelligent woman, who struggled as best she could with traumas, both childhood and adult, at a time
when there was little in the way of effective treatment.

By the end of 1892 Freud's practice had picked up and he was employing
the cathartic method with a number of patients. A physician colleague was
treating a young woman for a nasal infection and noted that she was easily
fatigued and depressed, and complained of loss of appetite. He referred
her to Freud, who saw her intermittently over the course of nine weeks.
He wrote up this treatment—which became the second full case presented
in *Studies*—under the name "Miss Lucy R." She was an English governess,
employed by a wealthy factory director to care for his two daughters following the death of his wife. In addition to her depression, there was also
a disturbance in her sense of smell; she could not rid herself of the odors

of "burnt pudding" and "cigar smoke," though she knew they were not in the air, and Freud astutely described how a psychological symptom like this may follow an actual physical illness, her nasal infection. Given her low status and lack of money—a stark contrast to Bertha Pappenheim, Anna von Lieben, and Fanny Moser—along with the mild nature of her disturbance, one wonders why Freud included her in *Studies*, because most of the patients in his practice had more serious and complex syndromes. The answer to this question has to do with two features of her case: his giving up the technique of hypnotic suggestion and, of greater significance, his description of repression as the major mechanism in the genesis of her symptoms.

Freud tried to hypnotize Miss Lucy, without success, so he conducted the whole treatment with her in a normal, waking state. Compared to his use of hypnotic suggestion with Frau Moser, this was an important step in the evolution of his technique. He did not allow her to speak freely but used what he came to call "the pressure technique." As he put it, "I decided to start from the assumption that my patients knew everything that was of any pathogenic significance and that it was only a question of obliging them to communicate it." He would put his hand on her forehead or take her head between his hands, and instruct her that, when he relaxed his pressure, something would come to mind related to her problems.

The unraveling of her symptoms showed an association between the troublesome odors and certain painful events—in Miss Lucy's case, trauma is probably too strong a word; psychological conflict is more apt. She was secretly in love with her employer and hoped that she would one day take the place of his late wife. She also told Freud that she was deeply attached to his two daughters in her role as substitute mother. Her marital aspirations put her at odds with the other servants, who "joined in a little intrigue against me and said all sorts of things against me." Her employer did not back her up when she complained to him about this, and she contemplated leaving her position. Some further actions of his, including an angry outburst, made it clear that her hopes that he would marry her would come to naught, and certain specific events involved in this disappointment occurred when some pudding had burnt and cigars were being smoked, hence the association of her disappointed hopes and her sadness at the possible loss of the children whom she loved with the noxious odors.

Freud confronted her, saying,

> I believe that really you are in love with your employer, the Director, though perhaps without being aware of it yourself, and that you have a secret hope of taking their mother's place in actual fact. And then we must remember the sensitiveness you now feel towards the servants, after having lived with them peacefully for years. You're afraid of their having some inkling of your hopes and making fun of you. She answered in her usual laconic fashion: "Yes, I think that's true"—But if you knew you loved your employer why didn't you tell me?—"I didn't know—or rather I didn't want to know. I wanted to drive it out of my head and not think of it again; and I believe latterly I have succeeded. . . . And then I am only a poor girl and he is such a rich man of good family. People would laugh at me if they had any idea of it."

Two days after his unraveling of the meanings of her symptoms, she was cheerful, and the troublesome odors and her depression were gone. She told him she was still in love with her employer, knew nothing would come of it, and would keep the thoughts and feelings to herself. Freud encountered her four months later at a summer resort; she was in "good spirits" and assured him that her recovery had been maintained.

At one point in his discussion of Miss Lucy, Freud stated, "An idea must be intentionally repressed from consciousness," and he later added, "The splitting of consciousness in these cases of acquired hysteria is accordingly a deliberate and intentional one." This fits with Miss Lucy's statement that she "didn't want to know, [or] wanted to drive it out of my head and not think of it again." It is an early appearance of Freud's concept of repression as a willful process and contrasts with Breuer's view of dissociation, or the splitting of the self, as an involuntary act that occurs following severe trauma.

Freud characterized repression as a deliberate means of dealing with psychological conflict, which then takes on an unconscious life of its own. Patients knew and didn't know what was in their minds; his treatment consisted of "obliging" them to communicate it. Repression, related to relatively mild conflicts such as Miss Lucy's, certainly occurs. The conflicts are close to awareness, and the emotions and symptoms, in contrast to those found in Bertha Pappenheim and Fanny Moser, are circumscribed and relatively mild. This kind of repression stands in marked contrast to the splitting of the self or dissociation that occurs in cases of severe trauma. The distinction between repression and dissociation, touched on in the cases in *Studies*, foreshadowed what would shortly become a major disagreement between Freud and Breuer.

In August 1893, shortly after his treatment of Miss Lucy, Freud was on his summer vacation in the mountains when he was approached by a young woman who, knowing he was a doctor, described her symptoms: shortness of breath, pains in her head, a crushing feeling on her chest, and the frightening image of an angry male face that she could not identify. She also felt that "someone's standing behind me and going to catch hold of me all at once." The feelings were so strong when they came upon her that she thought she was going to die. She was an eighteen-year-old innkeeper's daughter, whom Freud treated in a single session. Her real name was Aurelia Kronich, and under the name "Katharina" she became his third full case in *Studies*.

Freud correctly assumed that she was describing an anxiety attack and set about questioning her, telling her that, when her symptoms first appeared, "you must have seen or heard something that very much embarrassed you, and that you'd much rather not have seen." Aurelia responded that her symptoms had first appeared two years earlier when she looked through a window and discovered her "uncle" and "cousin" engaged in sexual intercourse. In reality, the uncle was her father, as Freud revealed in a footnote added to the case over thirty years later. When Aurelia saw them, she was so upset she couldn't catch her breath and "there was a hammering and buzzing in [her] head." This accounted for two of her symptoms, but Freud persevered, and she then told him that the sight of her father and cousin was so upsetting because it reminded her of sexual advances made by her father two years previously, when she was fourteen. The crushing feeling in her chest represented his body pressing on her as, in a drunken state, he attempted to have sex with her. She subsequently told her mother about this, which led to angry quarrels between the parents and, eventually, a divorce. Her father blamed her for the breakup of the marriage and "gave way to a senseless rage against me. . . . His face would get distorted with rage and he would make for me with his hand raised. . . . The face I always see now is his face when he was in a rage."

The case is a concise demonstration of the way traumatic experiences are expressed in physical symptoms and the relief the patient feels when the meaning of the symptoms is brought to consciousness. Although in his description Freud made clear the connection between the sexual scenes and attacks and Aurelia's symptoms, he did not appreciate the full traumatic effect of a father's attempted molestation of a fourteen-year-old girl, but rather claimed that "a mere suspicion of sexual relations calls up the affect of anxiety in virginal individuals." This was no "mere suspicion," but an attempted rape by a drunken father that subsequently put the young girl in the middle of an angry divorce. We see here an early example of Freud minimizing the effects of trauma and real events.

Freud never saw Aurelia again, so he had no way of knowing if his one-time treatment produced lasting change. Information uncovered subsequently fills out the case. The father, a heavy drinker, was a sexual predator who pursued every waitress, maid, and whatever other girl he could get his hands on. He was well known in the small mountain community for this, so the divorce was not only a result of Aurelia's revelations. He subsequently lived in a common-law marriage with the cousin whom he was caught with, and they had four children. Aurelia married a man who managed forests for a wealthy landowner and settled in Hungary, where she had six children who lived and another five or six who were stillborn or lost in miscarriages.

———

The last full case that Freud presented in *Studies* he called "Fraulein Elisabeth von R." (in reality Ilona Weiss), whom he saw in late 1892. Her condition had features in common with both Bertha Pappenheim and Miss Lucy. Freud's treatment of this young woman showed him at his best; he characterized it as "the first full-length analysis of a hysteria undertaken by me [and] one of the hardest that I had ever undertaken." He largely dispensed with hypnosis—there is none of the "wiping away" of symptoms and memories that he attempted with Frau Moser—and although he employed the pressure technique some of the time, as he had with Miss Lucy, he was much less concerned with the rapid removal of Ilona's symptoms. For the most part he let her talk about whatever came to mind. As he put it, "This procedure was one of clearing away the pathogenic psychical material layer by layer, and we liked to compare it with the technique of excavating a buried city." In addition, although he eventually "solved" the riddle of her hysteria, he allowed her to go over the material in different ways, took time with her, and stressed the therapeutic effect of emotional expression along with intellectual insight.

Ilona Weiss, twenty-four years old when Freud first saw her, was the youngest of three daughters of a prosperous Hungarian family. She was particularly close to her father, who treated her as the son he never had, a friend with whom he could share his ideas. At the same time,

> he did not fail to observe that her mental constitution was on that account departing from the ideal which people like to see realized in a girl. He jokingly called her "cheeky" and "cock-sure," and warned her against being too positive in her judgments and against her habit of regardlessly telling people the truth, and he often said she would find it hard to get a husband. She was in fact greatly discontented with being a girl. She was full of ambitious plans. She wanted to study or to have a musical training, and she was indignant at the idea of having to sacrifice her inclinations and her freedom of judgment by marriage.

Like Bertha Pappenheim, Ilona struggled with the restrictions placed on women, though her parents seem to have been more benign than Bertha's. Freud was mainly sympathetic to Ilona, but his prejudices toward women show through a few times, such as when he notes "the independence of her nature which went beyond the feminine ideal and found expression in a considerable amount of obstinacy, pugnacity and reserve."

Like Bertha's and Fanny Moser's, Ilona's family history was suffused with illness, death, and loss. First her father developed a heart condition and died, then her mother had a serious operation on her eyes and was confined to bed for a lengthy period, and finally, her middle sister died of heart failure. "In all these troubles and in all the sick-nursing involved, the largest share had fallen to our patient." She slept in her father's room for eighteen months, tending to him until his death, and cared for her mother for a lengthy period. The father's death brought hard times to the family (loss of income, social isolation), made more difficult by the mother's increasing ill health. Ilona worked hard to alleviate their plight but felt "acutely her helplessness, her inability to afford her mother a substitute for the happiness she had lost. . . . Unreconciled to her fate, embittered by the failure of all her little schemes for re-establishing the family's former glories, with those she loved dead or gone away . . . she had lived for eighteen months in almost complete seclusion with nothing to occupy her but the care of her mother." It was out of her isolation and the deaths and illnesses that Ilona's symptom emerged: pains in her legs which, at their worst, made it impossible for her to walk. From being the caretaker of others, she became the family invalid.

Freud brought all these traumatic experiences into the open and encouraged Ilona to freely express the emotions associated with them. He was astute in describing how tending to a sick or dying loved one leads to the holding back of feelings of grief and how this strangulated affect plays its role in symptom formation. He discovered a specific source for one of her leg pains: Her father had rested his leg on her thigh every morning as she changed the bandage on his swelling. But this was only a precipitating cause, and Freud was intent on tracking down the deeper source and meaning of her symptoms. He spent a great deal of time getting her to recall when the pains first started. The first significant memory was of an enjoyable evening she spent with a young man whom she found attractive, only to return home to find her father in a worse condition; she "reproached herself most bitterly for having sacrificed so much time to her own enjoyment."

This was the first appearance of a psychological conflict between her own desire for love and happiness with a man and her overweening sense of duty. Freud was largely sympathetic about this and "encouraged her to go to a party at which she might once more come across the friend of her youth." He focused on her need for a loving partner and found a more significant version in her attraction to the husband of her middle sister. Her special affection for this brother-in-law was obvious to those who knew them, including her own mother. When the young man first came to the house he mistook Ilona for her "somewhat insignificant looking sister," and they struck up a lively conversation. On another occasion, her sister felt unwell, so she and the brother-in-law joined a group for a walk, during which they "discussed every kind of subject, among them the most intimate ones . . . and a desire to have a husband like him became very strong in her." This precipitated the first appearance of her leg pains and difficulty walking, which she initially put down to the strain of the walk. When Freud asked about this, she was able to speak of the contrast between her own loneliness and her married sister's happiness.

The final conflict occurred when this sister eventually succumbed to a heart condition. Ilona and her mother arrived at her death bed and the thought "now forced itself irresistibly upon her once more, like a flash of lightning in the dark: 'Now he is free again and I can be his wife'." This thought came to Ilona herself; it is not one of Freud's guesses or reconstructions. Once again she was confronted with the conflict between her own wish for love and her guilt about a dead family member. As Freud put it, "This girl felt towards her brother-in-law a tenderness whose acceptance into consciousness was resisted by her whole moral being. She succeeded in sparing herself the painful conviction that she loved her sister's husband, by inducing physical pains in herself instead." This discovery had a "shattering effect on the poor girl," and she and Freud struggled for some time with her acceptance of the truth of this warded-off idea. He attempted to console her, stressing that she was not "responsible" for her feelings and that the conflict itself was evidence of her "moral character." There was a good deal of what would later be called "working through" of the conflict, with much open expression of emotion. Eventually Ilona accepted the truth, aided by Freud's "friendly interest in her present circumstances."

Freud ended his report by describing how he saw Ilona at a private ball some two years later. She whirled past him in a lively dance, her leg pains and difficulty walking obviously gone. He also heard that she had "married someone unknown to me." The only further evidence about her comes from an interview with her daughter conducted many years later. She reported that her mother's marriage was a happy one and that her mother had told her that Freud was "just a young, bearded nerve specialist they sent me to [who tried] to persuade me that I was in love with my brother-in-law, but that wasn't really so."

I find the evidence persuasive that Freud's work with Ilona was helpful and that the memory reported by her daughter, denying the insight her mother had reached during her treatment, is not unusual for someone who does not care to re-experience a painful time of her life. Ilona's case contained traumas—illnesses, deaths, and losses—and a conflict between her wish for a loving partner and the severe conscience that led her to sacrifice her life to care for others, both of which would have led to cut-off affective states, which were helped by the catharsis that Freud encouraged. Her disturbed condition was alleviated by the combination of insight and the unblocking of thoughts, memories, and feelings. In addition, throughout the treatment Freud was a largely supportive and sympathetic figure. He spoke of the "interest shown in her by the physician, the understanding of her which he allows her to feel and the hopes of recovery he holds out to her" and, later, "abreaction [the expression of blocked emotion] certainly did her much good. But I was able to relieve her still more by taking a friendly interest in her present circumstances." So, although his own summary emphasized the overcoming of repression, his full account of the case made clear that his supportive and sympathetic attitude also played an important part in her recovery.

———

Freud's approach to treatment changed a good deal in the five years between 1887 and 1892. In the first treatment that he reported in full, that of Fanny Moser, he used hypnotic suggestion in an authoritative manner, attempting to banish her troubling emotions and memories. This produced only temporary relief, and hypnotism played no part in the treatment of Lucy R. and Aurelia Kronich. By the time he treated Ilona Weiss, there was no attempt to wipe out her memories; on the contrary, he worked at getting her to recover her thoughts and express them fully. Although the change in his treatment technique is important, of greater significance is what these patients reveal about the causes of neuroses. In Freud's description, it is abundantly clear that all of them suffered from disturbing life events—from the severe traumatic deaths and persecution of Fanny Moser, to the attempted rape by her own father of the fourteen-year-old Aurelia Kronich, to the severe and punitive consciences (a result, in part, of the social constraints placed on women) that led Bertha Pappenheim and Ilona Weiss to sacrifice their own lives to care for family members. Freud presented a picture of all these events, but one also sees the beginnings of his sexual theories making their appearance, in remarks about Frau Moser's supposed "sexual abstinence" and Aurelia's "virginal anxiety." This substitution of sexuality for trauma and other actual events became more apparent in his final chapter in *Studies*.

CHAPTER SIX

Among the Afflicted

> *No one can keep account of damage done to himself. We imagine we have absorbed the shock, the harm, but we have merely caged it, and not in a strong cage either. It waits within the bars for a signal. And however long the wait may be, the leap is always unerring; a man can after twenty years be struck by a horror he thought he had forgotten and it will be green and fresh as ever.*
> BARRY UNSWORTH
> *Sacred Hunger,* 1992

Josef Breuer and Sigmund Freud had been friends for a number of years, yet their differences were mounting as they wrote *Studies on Hysteria.* Their divergent ideas were clearest in the final two chapters of the book—Breuer's "Theoretical" and Freud's "The Psychotherapy of Hysteria"—which they wrote independently. The departure in their views, only suggested in the earlier case reports, now began to take more substantial form. More and more, Freud emphasized his view of repression as a willful pushing of ideas from one's mind, whereas Breuer argued for his concept of a "hypnoid state," which occurred automatically and unconsciously in cases of severe hysteria. These differences had important implications for treatment: Freud, in his future cases, would "oblige" his patients to reveal what they were holding back, whereas Breuer's inclination would have been to establish a collaborative relationship that allowed the traumatic material to emerge at the patient's own pace. There was also a growing dispute over whether hysteria and other neuroses could all be attributed to a single cause—a position that Freud was beginning to expound—or had distinct roots in each individual patient. A close examination of the other chapters in *Studies* will illustrate the differences between the two authors.

"Preliminary Communication" was originally published as a journal article in 1893 and then become the first chapter in *Studies*. It is a small gem that clearly and succinctly presents a number of the concepts and methods that later formed the foundation of psychoanalytic theory and practice. In this article/chapter Breuer and Freud stated their belief that "hysterical attacks" were the result of traumas that had been bottled up; the emotions associated with them were not "abreacted"—that is, not given full or "cathartic" expression—and for this reason they revealed their presence through symptoms. The two doctors came to believe that people are not conscious of the relationship between the traumas they have suffered and their symptoms. They reasoned that this may be due to a deliberate avoidance of unpleasant memories, but that more often people have "no suspicion of the causal connection between the precipitating event and the pathological phenomenon." They noted that frequently the traumatic event took place in childhood, and the resulting symptoms had persisted for many years. Crucial here, of course, is their idea of unconscious mental life: that a person has no awareness of powerful emotional events, traumas, or the origins and meaning of his or her disturbance.

Hypnosis could be used to demonstrate the existence of unconscious processes, such as when a subject was put in a trance and told that he would perform some act when awakened but would have no memory of why he was doing it. It was also the starting place for the treatment of hysterical patients, as seen in the cases of Bertha Pappenheim and Fanny Moser, and it took Freud some time to work his way free of this procedure. In "Preliminary Communication" the two authors asserted, "As a rule it is necessary to hypnotize the patient and to arouse his memories under hypnosis of the time at which the symptom made its first appearance." Breuer used the term "hypnoid state" to refer to what he also called a "splitting of the mind," "double conscience," or "dissociation," a condition in which severely traumatic events do not register consciously because they are too frightening or emotionally overwhelming. The person is not aware of such events, but they persist as physical and emotional states in a split-off part of the mind; they do not become part of one's continuous sense of self. Of course such phenomena need not be tied to hypnotism, so calling them "hypnoid states" was misleading; "dissociation" from one's conscious sense of self would have been more accurate.

Breuer and Freud's understanding of the genesis of hysterical symptoms led to a treatment, "the cathartic method," in which patients were taken back to the origin of their hysteria and encouraged to re-experience the events associated with its onset. As they explained,

> Each individual hysterical symptom immediately and permanently disappeared when we had succeeded in bringing clearly to light the memory of the event by which it was provoked and in arousing its accompanying affect, and when the patient had described that event in the greatest possible detail and had put the affect into words. Recollection without affect almost invariably produces no result.

Although the general model presented here was of enormous value, it was much more difficult to achieve cures in practice than this statement implies. The patients' symptoms did not always "immediately and permanently" disappear, though the retrieval of memories and cathartic re-experiencing could be helpful.

Breuer and Freud used the concept of "strangulated affect" to describe what happens when a person does not have a direct or adequate emotional response to a traumatic, threatening, or disturbing event. Their examples covered a range of experiences, from the person who suffers a loss but is unable to cry or grieve, to one who is injured but must swallow the insult rather than "blow off steam," express anger, or take revenge. "An injury that has been repaid, even if only in words, is recollected quite differently from one that has to be accepted." They also noted that experiences that become unconscious are cut off from "the great complex of associations." When a traumatic or emotionally injurious event exists outside of awareness, it retains its original form and power:

> It may therefore be said that the ideas which have become pathological have persisted with such freshness and affective strength because they have been denied the normal wearing-away processes by means of abreaction and reproduction in states of uninhibited association. [As one example they note how] . . . a person's memory of a humiliation is corrected by his putting the facts right, by considering his own worth, etc. In this way a normal person is able to bring about the disappearance of the accompanying affect through the process of association.

Freud and Breuer made clear that, although one can speak of a trauma as if it is a single entity, more typically a series of related events have a cumulative effect. The cases in *Studies* certainly bear this out; behind the psychological disturbance of most of the patients lies a complex group of traumatic and conflict-laden occurrences and relationships that cannot be reduced to a single event. They also noted that the connection between the cause and the symptom may be a symbolic one. For example, "A neuralgia may follow upon mental pain or vomiting upon a feeling of moral disgust."

Dreams were mentioned briefly as another example of an unconscious, symbolic phenomenon. The childhood origins of symptoms were also just noted, though several of the cases provided the historical background of the patients and the connection of their early experiences to their breakdowns. Breuer did no more with the symbolic meaning of symptoms, dreams, and the importance of childhood experience, but Freud, of course, incorporated all these as central parts of psychoanalysis in the years to come.

In a letter to his friend Wilhelm Fliess, written in December 1892—that is, shortly before the article version of "Preliminary Communication" was published—Freud remarked, "It has cost enough in battles with my esteemed partner," to which the translator adds that Freud's German term, translated as "esteemed partner," is "Herr Compagnon," which has a somewhat disdainful as well as humorous connotation. The two men disagreed about the weight Breuer gave to trauma and dissociation on the one hand, and Freud's growing emphasis on sexuality and repression on the other. The precipitating events of symptoms, described in "Preliminary Communication," are dissociated traumas and support Breuer's conceptions more than Freud's. In addition, sexuality does not appear in this chapter; the affective states at the root of the patient's disturbance are fright, anxiety, anger, grief, shame, and humiliation. Freud, as shown in his case presentations (most clearly in the case of Ilona Weiss), was beginning to move toward a theory that stressed the importance of sexual conflict. A short time later he argued that sexuality lies behind all the other troublesome emotions of psychological disturbance and gave increasing weight to repression, also called "defense," which he defined as a willful forcing of unacceptable thoughts and feelings from consciousness. As he stated in his final chapter in *Studies*:

> I willingly adhere to this hypothesis of there being a hypnoid hysteria. Strangely enough, I have never in my own experience met with a genuine hypnoid hysteria. . . . I am unable to suppress a suspicion that somewhere or other the roots of hypnoid and defense hysteria come together, and that there the primary factor is defense.

Breuer continued to see patients with various psychiatric complaints in the years after his work with Bertha Pappenheim but never again carried out a full cathartic treatment; for this reason, the discussion in his final chapter was more focused on general issues. He took up the work of other investigators of hysteria, such as Alfred Binet, Pierre Janet, and Paul Moebius, and sorted out the points of agreement and disagreement between his and Freud's ideas and theirs. He began by asserting, "Psychical processes will be dealt with in a language of psychology," an important idea that freed the discussion from previous theories, which defined hysteria as a neurological disease. At the same time, he discussed how many symptoms, although primarily psychological, also interact with somatic factors. For example, a physical injury that causes pain can be elaborated by the person and become a source of "hysterical pain."

The main focus of Breuer's discussion was the concept of the unconscious. In his chapter, "Theoretical," he sorted through the ways in which different experiences become unconscious. He considered, for example, whether boring or repetitive activities can lead a patient to drift off into states of reverie or daydreaming—such as Bertha Pappenheim's "private theater"—and wondered whether this was why so many women broke down when they were nursing loved ones for long periods of time. He concluded that states of reverie were not sufficient to explain most unconscious phenomena. He engaged with Freud's ideas about the role of sexuality and supported them, even asserting at one point "that the great majority of severe neuroses in women have their origin in the marriage bed." Such conflicts can arise in women, he noted, "of a refined organization who, though their sexual excitability is great, have an equally great moral purity and who feel that anything sexual is something incompatible with their ethical standards, something dirtying and smirching."

Despite his support of Freud's views on sexual conflict and repression, Breuer assigned greater weight to hypnoid states, which he saw as central to the role of the unconscious in "major" or "severe hysteria." In contrasting the hypnoid state with repression or defense he described the two ways in which emotionally laden ideas become unconscious: "The first is 'defense,' the deliberate suppression of distressing ideas which seem to the subject to threaten his happiness or self-esteem." This would fit his description of the woman caught between her "sexual excitability" and her "ethical standards." The second occurs "not because one does not want to remember the idea, but because one cannot remember it: because it originally emerged and was endowed with affect in states in respect of which there is amnesia in waking consciousness." Such states are characterized by overwhelming emotions such as terror and rage. An example from contemporary practice would be a young girl who feels herself split into two people, one of whom is up on the ceiling watching as her father sexually molests the "other" her. This is the kind of automatic dissociation of the personality that happens in cases of severe trauma. Thus, although Breuer gave credit to Freud's ideas of repression and defense, he also stated, "I am still of the opinion that hypnoid states are the cause and necessary condition of many, indeed of most, major and complex hysterias." Later he observed, "Alongside sexual hysteria we must at this point recall hysteria due to fright—traumatic hysteria proper—which constitutes one of the best known and recognized forms of hysteria."

A final source of the emerging conflict between the two men was whether hysteria, along with many other forms of neurosis, could be explained by a single overarching principle or had different causes in different cases. In a lecture he gave in 1895, Breuer said, "One point on which the speaker does not agree with Freud is the overvaluation of sexuality; Freud probably did not want to say that every hysterical symptom has a sexual background, but rather that the original root of hysteria is sexual. We do not yet see clearly; it remains only for the future, the masses of observations to bring full clarification to this question." Freud's reaction to this was to write about Breuer to his friend Fliess, "I think of the underhandedness with which he doled out praise . . . and the consideration which led him to express his picky objections to the essentials. . . . Again and again I am glad to be rid of him." By this time Freud was demanding complete agreement with his new, sweeping theory of sexuality and defense, and when this was not forthcoming from Breuer, he turned on him. In contrast, for Breuer it was a matter of scientific difference; as he stated at the end of his chapter, "Theoretical":

> The attempt that has been made here to make a synthetic construction of hysteria out of what we know of it today is open to the reproach of eclecticism, if such a reproach can be justified at all. There are so many formulations of hysteria . . . for so many excellent observers and acute minds have concerned themselves with hysteria. It is unlikely that any of their formulations was without a portion of the truth. A future exposition of the true state of affairs will certainly include them all and will merely combine all the one-sided views of the subject into a corporate reality. Eclecticism, therefore, seems to me nothing to be ashamed of.

This conclusion shows Breuer's openness to different theories and the contributions of other investigators, an approach that Freud would soon treat with disdain.

By 1895 Freud had accumulated considerable clinical experience, and the discussion in his chapter, "Psychotherapy of Hysteria," shows the development of a number of new ideas. At the same time, he was very focused on finding a sexual root at the base of *every* neurosis, something that was to plague psychoanalysis for many years. An early version of the concept of "transference" was outlined in this chapter, which he defined as a "false connection." As an example, he described a patient who, many years earlier, had wished that a man she was talking with would give her a kiss. In a session, a similar wish arose in relation to Freud, which then blocked her work in the next session. It was only when he was able to "discover the obstacle and remove it" that the therapy could proceed.

Early in his chapter Freud argued that "sexual factors" were central to the acquisition of "the neuroses in general." He then reinterpreted each of his four long cases in terms of sexual causation. Frau Moser's anxiety had "originated from sexual abstinence and had become combined with hysteria." What he first presented as a guess about her "abstinence" in the original case report was now stated as a fact. Freud said that Miss Lucy "had an unmistakable sexual aetiology." This was true only if one substitutes sexuality for unrequited love. During her therapy, when Freud asked her, "Were you ashamed of loving a man?" she responded, "Oh no, I'm not unreasonably prudish. We're not responsible for our feelings, anyhow." This does not seem to support his assertion of an unmistakable sexual etiology. Aurelia Kronich, who was violently molested by her father, was now "nothing less than a model of what I have described as 'virginal anxiety'," referring back to his supposition that the "mere suspicion of sexual relations calls up the affect of anxiety in virginal individuals." In the case of Ilona Weiss, he was not able to investigate a "sexual neurosis" but suspected that it was there nonetheless. He also referred to twelve additional cases that purportedly supported his claim of sexual causation but did not provide any details about them. As one looks over these four cases, as well as those of Bertha Pappenheim and Anna von Lieben, the evidence supporting Freud's claim for the centrality of "sexual factors" is simply not there.

———

In addition to the five cases reported at length in *Studies*, ten patients were briefly mentioned at different places in the text. Breuer described a twelve-year-old boy who complained of a sore throat, wouldn't eat, and was subject to vomiting. No physical cause was found, and he finally confessed that, while walking home from school, he had stopped at a public urinal, where a man exposed himself and asked him to take his penis in his mouth. The boy had run off in fear, and his symptoms—which represented feelings of disgust—began at that point, only to vanish when he was able to speak with Breuer about the frightening experience. Breuer also described an attractive teenage girl whose anxiety resulted from "a number of more or less brutal attempts made on her. . . . A young man had attacked her and she had escaped from him with difficulty." He also mentioned a little girl whose convulsions were traced, under hypnosis, to "being chased by a savage dog," as well as the case of a man whose employer "abused him in the street and hit him with a stick." The man's symptoms—which represented his bottled up rage—returned when he "failed to obtain satisfaction for his maltreatment" in court.

Freud briefly described six patients in whom the "sexual factors" consisted of actual assaults and molestations, as well as traumas that did not involve sexuality. "Matilda H." was depressed, irritable, and lethargic. Under hypnosis, her symptoms were traced to the breaking off of her engagement when she and her mother discovered "unwelcome" things about her fiancé. She was working through this deep loss bit by bit over the course of a year.

"Fraulein Rosalia H." was a singer whose throat became constricted, seriously compromising her ability to perform. Her father "brutally ill-treated his wife and children" and tried to rape Rosalia. She made unsuccessful attempts to protect her younger siblings from him. The constriction of her throat came from her efforts to "suppress her hatred and contempt" of him. In his treatment, Freud was able to get her to reproduce the traumatic experiences and encouraged her to vent her anger at her father and tell him the truth.

Freud also mentioned "a gifted lady" who had "nursed to the end three or four of those whom she loved . . . and reached a state of complete exhaustion." The grief she was not able to express during the long period of caring for others overtook her later in the form of "outbursts of weeping" on the anniversaries of the deaths or on other occasions associated with her losses. He referred to her condition as "abreaction in arrears."

Freud also described the case of a girl who suffered from a nervous cough for six years. He helped her describe the onset of her symptom at age fourteen, when her dog died. She further revealed her feeling that the dog was the only one in the world who loved her and that after he died she was quite alone. Freud relieved her symptom, but it recurred when she received the news of the death of an uncle who seemed to be the only member of her family with any feeling for her. Another young girl had symptoms of waking each morning in a stuporous condition, with her limbs rigid and her tongue sticking out. Freud was able to discover that when she was younger, she had been sexually molested each night by her governess. Finally, he reported the case of a "lady who had suffered for many years from obsessions and phobias." He took her through a series of associations that eventually unearthed a memory from age ten, when her older sister "went raving mad one night" and had to be taken away. Further investigation revealed that "they slept in one room and on a particular night they had both been subjected to sexual assaults by a certain man."

These sixteen patients—the five long cases plus Anna von Lieben and the ten who were briefly described—comprise the evidence on which Freud built his theory that "sexual factors" are the root of all forms of neurosis. True, several of the women and the young boy described by Breuer were subjected to sexual molestations and attempted rape, but these abusive acts were traumatic; they did not involve conflicts between sexual desires and conscience. In the case of Aurelia, Freud did not attribute her anxiety primarily to the attempted rape by her father but to the mere thought of sexuality in such a "virginal" girl. Ilona Weiss is the only one

of these patients who fits his theory of a repressed or defended sexual conflict, and that was not the only cause of her breakdown. Many of the other
women—Bertha Pappenheim, Fanny Moser, Ilona Weiss, the "gifted lady,"
and the girl whose beloved dog died—were experiencing blocked grief following the loss of loved ones. Other factors implicated in their neuroses
included the great restrictions placed on women in the nineteenth-century
Austro-Hungarian Empire, which were at the heart of Bertha Pappenheim's breakdown; clear in the case of Ilona Weiss, who chafed at not being able to do the things men could do; and no doubt present in most, if
not all, of the other women, who could not help but be harmed by their
second-class positions in society.

Additional factors played important roles in the disturbances of these
patients, including betrayal by intimates and family members, disappointed hopes, loss of love, and—particularly prominent—the disturbing
effects of overly severe moral standards, which Breuer referred to as
"pathological conscientiousness." The latter was what led so many of these
women to stifle their emotions, to remain "polite," not to speak their
minds, or to devote themselves to the nursing and care of others to the
point of emotional collapse.

In his discussion of one of the cases in *Studies*, Freud stated, "It still
strikes me myself as strange that the case histories I write should read like
short stories and that, as one might say, they lack the serious stamp of
science." Far from being a defect, this quality gives a richness to Freud's
writing that takes it beyond the narrow theoretical constructions he
would increasingly promulgate. Although he attempted to promote his
theory of exclusive sexual causation, his descriptions of the cases are filled
with information that brings these women to life in all their complex in-
dividuality. As just one example, he noted that when Frau Moser came to
see him the second time, she "was often in tears for hours at a time." Although he made no attempt to explain this, the reader cannot help but be
moved. The information he himself provides permits us to see the many
sides of the lives and illnesses of his patients in addition to their sexuality. We are able to do this even though Freud was beginning to reject the
shattering effects of trauma and its attendant dissociation, and the many

other factors involved in the patients' breakdowns, as he attempted to en-compass everything in a single, sweeping theory.

This is the great mystery of Freud. After unearthing all the evidence of trauma, loss, abuse, moral self-reproach, and suppression of women, why did he neglect all these facts and completely invest himself in a theory of sexual conflict and repression? The answer to this puzzle will also explain why, after many years of friendship and collaboration, he broke off his re-lationship with Breuer and took up with Wilhelm Fliess.

CHAPTER SEVEN

Freud's "Only Other"

> Friendship, popularly represented as something
> simple and straightforward—in contrast to
> love—is perhaps no less complicated, requiring
> equally mysterious nourishment; like love too,
> bearing also within its embryo inherent seeds of
> dissolution.
>
> ANTHONY POWELL
> *A Dance to the Music of Time,* 1966

S tudies on Hysteria was favorably reviewed by leading psychiatrists such as Eugen Bleuler in Switzerland, the sex researcher Havelock Ellis in England, and neurologists and other medical men in Germany and Austro-Hungary. It even received positive notice in literary circles. Adolf Strümpell, a professor of neurology in Leipzig, wrote, "Both authors have tried to give us, with much adroitness and psychological penetration, a deeper insight into the mental condition of hysterics, and their statements offer much that is interesting and stimulating." There was also criticism, some justified and some reflecting old prejudices such as the inappropriateness of probing into the sexual lives of women. But, on the whole, the book was recognized as the groundbreaking work that it was. Nevertheless, Freud was obsessed with the criticism. He required nothing less than total praise, an early sign of his creation of the myth that those in authority rejected his work, that he labored, in the face of opposition, in a state

of "splendid isolation" as he created psychoanalysis on his own, also ig-
noring his fruitful collaboration with Josef Breuer.

Breuer had never been a heroic model for Freud in the way Ernst Brücke
and Jean-Martin Charcot were, even though his scientific achievements
were on par with Brücke's and his work with "hysteria" perhaps more significant than Charcot's. In Freud's eyes, his mentor's very kindness and
modesty disqualified him for this role. Breuer was a caring, approachable,
parental figure, who had the potential to arouse a threatening sense of
helplessness and dependency in Freud. Having identified with military heroes as a child, as a budding physician Freud strove to become a famous
man in his new field; in his role as psychologist he imagined himself the
equivalent of Newton or Darwin.

In his quest for fame, Freud turned on Breuer and cut him out of his
life entirely just a few years after *Studies* was published. Breuer's daughter-
in-law, who joined the family in 1906, reported that her father-in-law rarely
spoke about his earlier relationship with Freud—though he followed his
publications with interest—even though the two men lived close to each
other in Vienna and had medical colleagues in common. She recalled an
incident many years later when Breuer, by then an old man, was walking in
the street; he saw Freud approaching and instinctively opened his arms in
greeting. Freud passed by as if he did not see him.

Wilhelm Fliess, in contrast, was not a cautious scientist, nor was he held
back by modesty; his own theories were as sweeping as Freud's were becoming. The Berlin doctor, who was two years younger than Freud, was
first introduced to him (ironically, by Breuer) at a lecture Freud gave in
1887, eight years before the publication of *Studies*. What was it about Fliess
that so aroused Freud's admiration? His new idol had broad interests and
was described as "fascinating" by many who knew him. Even the skeptical
Breuer was impressed by his ideas. In addition to his work as a doctor,
Fliess espoused wide-ranging biological theories that some physicians and
scientists saw as great discoveries and others viewed with skepticism. The
breadth and novelty of his theories, their skeptical reception by the medical establishment, and the fact that he was Jewish were all features that
strengthened Freud's identification with Fliess.

Fliess's theories were based on two suppositions, one involving the nose and the other what he termed "male and female periods." He began with the fact that there is an anatomical similarity between nasal and genital tissue and then expanded this to what he called "the nasal reflex neurosis." Problems with the nasal membranes and bones were held responsible for symptoms and diseases throughout the body: headaches; pains in the abdomen, arms, and legs; coronary symptoms; asthma; gastrointestinal problems; and, of special interest to Freud, such reproductive disturbances as miscarriages, dysmenorrhea, and cramping. The nasal reflex theory led to simple treatments; for example, sexual difficulties or heart symptoms could be cured by applying cocaine to the nasal membranes or be treated with surgery on the nose.

Fliess's second theory also began with a fact, the twenty-eight-day female menstrual cycle. From this he postulated a "male cycle" of twenty-three days (which does not in fact exist) and developed a theory of "critical dates." The twenty-eight- and twenty-three-day cycles were part of his conception of "bisexuality"; the first defined the "female period" and the second the "male." According to Fliess, these sexual periods determined the stages of human growth, illness, and death; they operated throughout the animal kingdom and connected biological events to the movements of the sun, moon, and stars. Armed with knowledge of a person's birthday and other critical dates, a great deal could be predicted with seeming mathematical certainty, using the numbers 28 and 23, with the later addition of the number 5 (28 minus 23), which could be added or subtracted as needed to make the calculations fit.

Fliess's theories began with small possibilities—similarities between nasal and genital tissue, the periodicity of some biological phenomena—and then wildly expanded them. The state of scientific medicine at the time made his ideas more plausible than they seem today, but not by much. The problem was his grandiosity, his need to move from some minor observation to the most wide-ranging claims. Many patients with medical and psychological problems were eager to grasp at such ideas and the treatments associated with them, especially when they were stated with conviction by a charismatic physician. Perhaps some of the patients whose noses he treated surgically felt better as a result of their association with a powerful doctor; certainly the "local application" of cocaine—which Fliess frequently prescribed—would relieve pain and lift their spirits. However, at least one patient—Emma Eckstein, who was also in therapy with Freud—almost died from an infection following Fliess's incompetent operation on her nose.

Looked at now, Fliess appears to have been one in a long line of medical quacks whose need for fame led them to create totalistic theories and treatments. And he was seen as such by perceptive critics in his own time. Ry—the pen name of a reviewer of Fliess's 1897 *The Relationship between the Nose and the Female Sexual Organs*—could discover only one worthwhile statement in the entire book: that labor pains could be treated with the application of cocaine to the nose. Even this finding does not support Fliess's theory. It is not the nose per se that is important; cocaine would be effective however it got into the bloodstream, as Freud, who used to take it orally, should have known. Ry characterized the book as "mystical nonsense" and "disgusting gobbledygook" that "has nothing to do with medicine or natural science." Out of loyalty to his friend, Freud, who had no foreknowledge of the review, withdrew in protest from the editorial board of the journal that published it.

Ry's appraisal of Fliess's theories revealed them for what they were: overblown speculations, without foundation in observation, and therapeutically worthless, if not harmful. Yet despite such criticism, Freud saw these ideas as bold and revolutionary. Fliess's theories seemed to provide a bridge between Freud's previous neuroanatomical research and his new involvement in psychology; they dealt with tissues, bones, drugs, numbers, and surgery, rather than ephemeral thoughts, memories, emotions, and psychotherapy. Struggling with the uncertainty of his new approach, Freud took comfort in what he saw as the solidity of Fliess's work.

Another source of Freud's attraction to Fliess was his concern with sexuality and bisexuality; there was a great deal in their letters about these topics, ostensibly as areas of scientific research. Freud saw his colleague as someone who was not afraid of these subjects at a time when they were still shrouded in taboos, making him a courageous ally. In addition, the theory of "universal biological bisexuality" legitimized his personal attraction to his friend. However, the principal appeal of Fliess's theories was the scope and power they seemed to possess; he appeared to be a great man whose discoveries would shake up the world. As Freud wrote to his colleague, referring to the astronomer Johannes Kepler, whose laws of planetary motion had established his fame as a scientist, "I hope the path you have taken will lead you even farther and even deeper, and that as the new Kepler you will unveil the ironclad rules of the biological mechanism to us. Indeed you have your calling in life."

Fliess's theoretical imperialism was the principal reason Freud took up with him and dropped the cautious Breuer. His Berlin friend seemed like a bold scientific genius, a "new Kepler," which made him a model for Freud, who would in turn be the Isaac Newton of the mind. They would be "twins," one a great biologist and the other a great psychologist.

In his correspondence with Martha during their long engagement, Freud seemed to want to be with his beloved girl more than anything else. Yet just one year after they were married, he initiated the relationship with Fliess, and he eventually became more open with him than he was with his wife. Martha was safely ensconced at home and much taken up with the births and care of babies. Moreover, she was not interested in his work. He could talk with her sister Minna, now a fixture in the apartment, and with Breuer in the years before their break, but neither provided what he required: someone who would support his emerging drive to be a great man.

Freud's first letter to Fliess already contained the flattery and overvaluation that would become characteristic of their relationship:

> Esteemed friend and colleague: My letter of today admittedly is occasioned by business; but I must introduce it by confessing that I entertain hopes of continuing the relationship with you and that you have left a deep impression on me which could easily lead me to tell you outright in what category of men I place you.

Freud only wrote a few letters to Fliess during the first years of their friendship, but by 1892 he was writing more than one a month, and by the end of the century, as many as three per month. In addition to exchanging over three hundred letters—including drafts of theories and projects—they had meetings, or, as Freud called them, "congresses," some in Vienna, where Fliess's wife's family lived, and some without their families for two or three days in other cities. Their final meeting took place in the fall of 1900.

Over the years Freud's expressions of affection for Fliess grew ever more ecstatic. "Esteemed friend and colleague" became "Dear friend," then "Dearest friend," and finally, "Dearest Wilhelm," "My beloved friend," and my "Only Other." The more formal "sie" (German has two forms for the English "you") changed to the intimate "du," and the letters became more and more personal. In June 1892 Freud wrote, "I have had no opportunity other than in memory to refer back to the beautiful evening on which I saw you (du)." In September 1893 he wrote, "You altogether ruin my critical faculties and I really believe you in everything." Freud's love reached a peak in January 1896:

> Your kind should not die out, my dear friend; the rest of us need people like you too much. How much I owe you: solace, understanding, stimulation in my loneliness, meaning to my life that I gained through you, and finally even health that no one else could have given back to me. It is primarily through your example that intellectually I gained the strength to trust my judgment, even when I am left alone—though not by you—and, like you, to face with lofty humility all the difficulties that the future may bring. For all that, accept my humble thanks! I know that you do not need me as much as I need you, but I also know that I have a secure place in your affection.

The inflated praise that Freud bestowed on Fliess, the need for contact—and his unhappiness when his "only other" did not write back quickly—and the way his sense of worth depended on Fliess's interest in him and his ideas are all signs of someone in love. As the correspondence continued, Freud became increasingly intimate. He discussed the state of his marriage and sex life: "We are now living in abstinence; and you know the reasons for this as well."

They were also preoccupied with each other's health. Fliess twice operated on Freud's nose, and there are many references in the letters to their pains and mood swings (both of them suffered from severe headaches), as well as other complaints. Fliess was a great believer in the medicinal power of cocaine, further strengthening Freud's dependence on him and the drug he prescribed. Although what Fliess wrote about his own health is not known (his letters have not been recovered), from comments by Freud one senses that they used their roles as physicians to express caring interest in each other. For Freud, this reached its peak during the period when he was in real danger of a heart attack. He suffered symptoms that, as a physician, he knew were signs of heart disease. Breuer even confirmed the diagnosis, which, given the lack of adequate treatment at the time, had a dire prognosis. Freud desperately wished to believe that Fliess was a "magical healer" who could cure him of his condition. In April 1894, when he thought he would die, he wrote, "The children and wife are well; the latter is not a confidante of my death deliria." At this critical time, he told his friend about the most important fear in his life but did not even discuss it with Martha. Fortunately his symptoms were due to a blockage in a minor coronary artery, and he recovered.

Although Freud's drive for fame is clear, the question remains, why did he attempt to make sexuality the single "ironclad" law of what he imagined would be a great theory? He could have focused on trauma or stressed the significance of death and loss, which were more prevalent in the cases described in *Studies*. The answer lies in the twists and turns of the self-analysis that he began shortly after the completion of *Studies*.

CHAPTER EIGHT

Inventing a Universal "Scientific" Law

Creon: *Seek and ye shall find. Unsought goes*
  undetected.
Oedipus: *I will start afresh; and bring everything*
  into the light.
Jocasta: *Best live as best we may, from day to*
  day. Nor need this mother-marrying frighten
  you; many a man has dreamt as much.
                                  SOPHOCLES
                            Oedipus Rex, 429 BC

*T*hroughout the 1890s Freud experienced an irruption of disturbing psychological symptoms, many quite like those of his patients. His treatment of hysterics had immersed him in a world
of fright, sadness, suppressed rage, sexual conflict, and other intense emotional states, all of which were far removed from the controlled and imper-
sonal world of Ernst Brücke's physiology laboratory. He was married,
having sex with his wife, and by 1895 was the father of six children. He had
also coauthored *Studies on Hysteria*, his first significant psychological book.
But at this time his own anxiety, phobias, depression, and mood swings
resurfaced in ways they had not done since he was a small boy.

At first he tried to account for his and his patients' symptoms as arising from sexual conflicts. Early in his correspondence with Wilhelm Fliess he speculated about the role of such conflicts. In February 1893 he wrote, "It may be taken as a recognized fact that neurasthenia is a frequent consequence of an abnormal sexual life." In the same letter he speculated about "sexual exhaustion" as seen in "neurasthenia," the harmful effects of "incomplete intercourse in order to prevent conception," and the way "intolerance of the condom, extravaginal coitus, and coitus interruptus take their toll." He seemed particularly focused on the harm caused by the use of condoms, an idea he held onto for many years (as seen in the 1908 paper that contains a veiled account of his own marriage), and said that if some other means of birth control were not found, "society appears doomed to fall victim to incurable neuroses, which reduce the enjoyment of life to a minimum, destroy marital relations, and bring hereditary ruin on the whole coming generation."

Some of these notions reflected widely held ideas about sex; for example, that masturbation in both boys and girls produced all sorts of terrible diseases, or that hysteria in women was caused by insufficient sexual "discharge." The idea that women who did not experience orgasm solely from penetration (which research now shows is true for over 70 percent of women) were "hysteric" was more than two thousand years old, and Freud's belief that only "vaginal" orgasms were normal reflected this idea. It was less threatening to blame the symptoms of most of his patients, and his own, on sexual factors than to experience the emotions associated with their traumatic roots. There are only occasional references in the Fliess letters to traumas, deaths, and losses; in this way the focus on sexuality served as what Freud himself would call a defense.

But it was a defense of limited value. His disturbing symptoms persisted, and within a year or two after the publication of *Studies*, he embarked on his self-analysis, relying on his dreams as the vehicle. He attempted to do for himself what he was doing with his patients and uncovered many significant memories from his early years. By his own account, the impetus for the self-analysis was the death of his father in 1896 at the age of eighty-two. He wrote to Fliess, "By the time he died, his life

had long been over, but in my inner self the whole past has been reawak-
ened by this event. I now feel quite uprooted." Some years later, in a preface to the second edition of *The Interpretation of Dreams*, Freud referred to
his father's death as "the most important event, the most poignant loss, of
a man's life."

The passing of Freud's father was one of many deaths that set loose
the emotions associated with the loss of loved and admired figures. Josef
Paneth, his friend since their first year at the university, colleague in
Brücke's laboratory, and financial benefactor, died young, in 1890. Ernst
Fleischl von Marxow, a financial supporter and companion during the
nights of drug-inspired philosophizing in the early 1880s, died after
many years of physical and mental decline, in 1891. Brücke died in 1892,
and Jean Martin Charcot in 1893. Perhaps most troubling was the loss of
Josef Breuer, who did not die but was dropped by Freud. Breuer was the
most nurturing and supportive man in Freud's adult life, and although
he claimed he was glad to be rid of Breuer, the loss was a profound one.
All these losses aroused the anxiety and depression that had continued
to live in an isolated compartment of Freud's mind since earliest childhood. Ancient terrors and symptoms now came back with new vigor; the
deaths and losses did, in fact, "reawaken the whole past of his inner
self."

Beginning in late 1896 Freud's letters to Fliess detailed the discoveries of
the self-analysis, including the death of his infant brother Julius, the loss
of his mother's care and attention, his love for his nursemaid and her sudden disappearance, the onset of his travel phobia, and his disappointment
with his father.

In recollecting his early years, Freud wrote to Fliess about his nursemaid, who "told me a great deal about God Almighty and hell and . . . in-
stilled in me a high opinion of my own capacities." She was a vital
maternal figure who supported his early sense of importance and precocious intelligence. He further recalled, "I shall be grateful to the memory
of the old woman [she was, in fact, in her early forties] who provided me
at such an early age with the means for living and going on living. As you
see, the old liking is breaking through again today."

This memory, from the time when death and the fear of death suffused the family, shows the importance of this substitute mother in sustaining his will to live and also demonstrates his direct affection for her, a feeling that returned forty years later. This kind of open love—"the old liking is breaking through again today"—was almost never voiced in relation to his mother, Amalia. Then the nursemaid disappeared from his life. The feelings connected with her loss, along with all the other losses of those years, brought about a state of helplessness that was too much to bear; the other, defensive side of Freud came to the fore. In the same letter in which he discussed his memory of the nursemaid, he described another memory, or rather a "reconstruction" of one, in which "between two and two and a half years—my libido toward *matrem* was awakened, namely, on the occasion of a journey with her from Leipzig to Vienna, during which we must have spent the night together and there must have been an opportunity of seeing her *nudam*. . . . You yourself have seen my travel anxiety at its height."

Here Freud moved from the memories and feelings associated with his losses to speculation: He and his mother "must have spent the night together" and he "must have seen" his "*matrem*" "*nudam*." He connected his supposed sexual arousal at seeing his mother naked with one of his earliest fears, the travel phobia. But this was not an actual memory, and he used the distancing latinisms in place of direct experience: "*matrem*" and "*nudam*" in contrast to the way he spoke of his nursemaid. This was an early appearance of what would shortly become his theory of the Oedipus complex.

His self-analysis had led him to the traumas of his own childhood, and he was then pulled in two directions. He wanted to discover the truth about his own past, but as the self-analysis proceeded he was exposed to threatening memories from his early years: not seductions, in his case, but helplessness in the face of overwhelming losses. These threatening memories could be countered by a bold and original theory of hysteria and the neuroses that would affirm his strength and make him a great man, as he imagined Fliess to be. As he wrote to his friend, "The expectation of eternal fame was so beautiful, as was that of certain wealth, complete independence, travels, and lifting the children above the severe worries that robbed me of my youth. Everything depended upon whether or not hysteria would come out right."

The "sexual factors" that he found in his patients were a mix of traumatic events (seductions of children by maids, governesses, and older siblings, and often of girls by their fathers), conflicts between desire and conscience, and nontraumatic causes such as "abstinence" or speculations about "virginal anxiety." As he pursued his self-analysis he would have had to apply these ideas to himself as well as to his patients. But this proved too dangerous, so he invented a half-truth, the Oedipal theory, which he then used to account for his own neurosis as well as everyone else's. Sophocles's play was perfect in this regard because it contained many themes that resonated with Freud's life. Oedipus's father is a king who, unlike the failed Jacob, when ordered to get off the road ("Jew! Get off the pavement!") strikes back with violence. He is also (as Freud the psychoanalyst would become) a great solver of riddles. Like Sophocles's protagonist, Freud "will start afresh; and bring everything into the light."

In September 1897 Freud wrote to Fliess, "I no longer believe in my neurotica [the theory of sexual seduction]," giving as his reasons his inability to cure his patients with interpretations based on the theory, the belief that "there are no indications of reality in the unconscious," and the fact that too many respectable fathers ("not excluding my own") would have to be accused of being perverse.

It was at precisely this time, when he was re-experiencing his early traumas, that he turned away from the unbearable emotions associated with them and substituted his theory of the Oedipus complex. This was the pivotal event in his abandonment not just of the seduction theory but of the reality of childhood trauma in all its many forms. As he wrote to Fliess, "A single idea of general value dawned on me. I have found, in my own case too, the phenomena of being in love with my mother and jealous of my father, and I now consider it a universal event in early childhood."

Freud's substitution of his universal Oedipal theory for one based on real traumas was a mixture of truth and speculation. It revealed his wish for his mother's love and her loss to a rival, though he made the need for mother-infant attachment "sexual" and substituted his father for the many babies who took his place. At the same time, it made him into a warrior, a young Oedipus, in combat with a king. It also did away with real traumas, sexual or any other kind, and gave primary emphasis to instincts and fantasies. In this new theory, it was not what actually happened that was the source of fear, depression, and symptoms—"the worries that robbed me of my youth"—but rather the young child's drive for pleasure, Oedipal fantasies, and sexual wishes that conflicted with moral standards. In addition, the theory itself—immediately promoted to "universal" status—became Freud's bid for "eternal fame"; it would make him a great scientist.

Freud's reasons for abandoning the seduction theory do not stand up to scrutiny. The fact that his patients did not get well when he interpreted their seductions did not prove that the theory of childhood trauma was wrong, but rather that he had not found an effective form of treatment. His belief that "there are no indications of reality in the unconscious" was also mistaken. The unconscious world of dreams and fantasies extends in many directions, but there is always a starting place in reality. Finally, although it may have been difficult for Freud to believe in the prevalence of sexual abuse, it was not uncommon.

What is more, it was a mistake to look for a single cause for each patient's neurosis, because the psychological disturbances of the women discussed in *Studies* and of his other patients arose from a wide variety of factors. Ilona Weiss most closely fit Freud's theory of the conflict between romantic/sexual desire and conscience, though she also suffered the loss of a loved one and struggled against the limitations imposed on her because she was a woman. Such limitations and the death of her father were the major source of Bertha Pappenheim's breakdown. Death and loss were ubiquitous in the case of Fanny Moser, as were a harsh conscience (a feature found in many of these women) and persecution by her late husband's family. Prolonged caretaking of dying loved ones, seen in the cases of Bertha and Ilona, was also apparent in the brief description of the "gifted lady." Aurelia Kronich was sexually molested, as were the young boy in the public urinal and several of the women who were briefly mentioned in *Studies.* A man was publicly beaten by his employer and failed to get justice in court. Miss Lucy struggled with unrequited love and her low status as a governess. And almost all the women (the large majority of Freud's patients at this time were women) chafed under the strictures imposed on them because of their gender. There were many causes of the neuroses, but they were always something real, not Oedipal or any other kind of fantasy, and each person should have been understood as a unique individual in a specific familial-social context.

Freud's self-analysis followed a wavering course and, although he recovered crucial memories, he could not hold onto them or the insights they produced. He had Fliess to confide much of this to, but his friend was not really a supportive or understanding therapist (he would have done much better if he hadn't cut himself off from Breuer), so it really was a *self-analysis*, with all the limitations of such an endeavor, and although he made important gains, in the end Freud moved away from the effects of trauma and real events and placed ever greater stress on his grand theories.

Freud's account of the supposed failure of his seduction theory was retold in *On the History of the Psycho-Analytic Movement* (1914), in which he turned his disappointment into a victory:

> If hysterical subjects trace back their symptoms to traumas that are fictitious, then the new fact which emerges is precisely that they create such scenes in phantasy, and this psychical reality requires to be taken into account alongside practical reality. This reflection was soon followed by the discovery that these phantasies were intended to cover up the autoerotic activity of the first years of childhood, to embellish it and raise it to a higher plane.

There is an important truth here along with a serious distortion. Freud's retreat from the reality of trauma went hand in hand with his discovery of the significance of fantasy and "psychic reality," which he elaborated on in *The Interpretation of Dreams*. Highlighting the psychological significance of dreams was one of Freud's most original contributions. The fantasy world of children, especially, is where they work out their understanding of reality, where they experiment with solutions to all the puzzling/ exciting/frightening events that confront them. But the existence of this realm does not negate the disturbing effects of real events. Posing the issue in either/or terms—either children have actually been traumatized or their memories of such events spring from fantasy fueled by sexual instincts—is misleading. Fantasy is a crucial area of human experience, but it is always fantasy about something. In fact, it is precisely those events that arouse fear and helplessness—the ones people are least able to control by action in the world—that they attempt to master in their play, imagination, and dreams.

With his creation of a theory that seemed to explain everything about the neuroses—the "universal" Oedipus complex—Freud was on his way to becoming a great man, a "conquistador" as he later referred to himself. He had in effect returned to the solution of his late childhood, when he escaped from all the traumas and troubles in his family and imagined himself a heroic military leader. He no longer had any need for Fliess; they quarreled over who first used the concept of bisexuality, and the intimate correspondence of over thirteen years drifted to an end. At their last "congress" in 1900 Fliess, seeing that Freud did not really give any credit to his theories, broke off the relationship in anger.

Many of the dreams that Freud used in his self-analysis found a place in his next book, *The Interpretation of Dreams*, published in 1900. It was this book, as well as *Studies*, that drew his first followers to Vienna. Now on his own—with no Breuer and no Fliess—he was ready to launch psychoanalysis as an international movement, to realize his dream of undying fame.

CHAPTER NINE

Full Circle

> *My model for this process is probably that of Dr.*
> *Breuer, who did not shrink from seeking and find-*
> *ing the truth in the most nonsensical statements of*
> *a hysteric, whereby he had to rely both theoretically*
> *and technically on the hints and suggestions of the*
> *patient.*
>
> SANDOR FERENCZI
> *The Clinical Diary,* 1932

*S*tudies on Hysteria began a revolution in our understanding of human personality and psychological disturbance. It is a tightly packed work that contains the potential for expansion into new theories and methods of treatment. And it was Freud—largely on his own after betraying his senior collaborator—who carried forth this expansion. Although Breuer first discovered "the talking cure" in his treatment of Bertha Pappenheim, it was Freud who dropped hypnosis and suggestion and pushed the field in a number of fruitful directions. Unfortunately, as he did so a great deal was shunted aside.

Perhaps the most significant concept in *Studies*—one that Freud and Breuer agreed on—is unconscious motivation, along with the closely related idea that many symptoms and acts are not due to physical disease but have psychological meaning. They are disguised communications that the patient does not understand. Other areas about which they agreed were

early hints at the formative importance of family relationships and childhood experiences, dreams as meaningful productions, and the idea of
transference.

Their views on other topics put them at odds, however. Although they
began using what seemed like the same treatment approach, Breuer was always more of a collaborator; he and Bertha Pappenheim co-created the
"talking cure." Freud became ever more the analyst-authority, the one who
knows what is in the patient's unconscious and, when he or she did not
agree with his interpretations, took this as evidence of "resistance." In addition, as Freud's drive for fame grew, he needed a single, overarching law
to fulfill his wish to be a great man, and he fastened on sexual conflict and
the Oedipus complex. Breuer recognized that sexual conflicts were important for some patients, but he did not see them as the only cause of neurosis. He laid great stress on trauma and dissociation—"hypnoid
states"—especially in cases of severe hysteria. Freud, in contrast, minimized the significance of trauma and many other real experiences and
dropped dissociation, as he promulgated his theories of sexual drives, fantasies, and repression. As time passed he minimized the importance of
catharsis and the value of emotional expression and made psychoanalysis
evermore an insight-oriented, intellectual endeavor.

Another difference was Breuer's belief that they had not arrived at a full
understanding of neurosis and that the research of other investigators was
needed to supplement their understanding. As he stated in his final chapter
in *Studies*, "So many excellent observers and acute minds have concerned
themselves with hysteria. It is unlikely that any of their formulations was
without a portion of the truth." He not only collaborated with his patients but argued for acceptance of the findings of other workers in the
field. Freud eventually insisted that he had worked out a complete theory,
that he had discovered the universal "laws" of neurosis.

Following publication of *Studies*, Freud renamed Breuer's cathartic
method "psychoanalysis" and went on to develop it in many creative directions. He had completed his self-analysis—as much as such an endeavor
can ever be said to be complete—and he finished *The Interpretation of Dreams*
in 1899. He treated Ida Bauer in 1900; as "Dora" she became the subject of

the first extensive case study demonstrating his new psychoanalytic method. Even as he was writing *Interpretation*, he was collecting examples of human errors and mistakes, which he wove together into *The Psychopathology of Everyday Life*, published in 1901. This eventually became his most popular book, and the "Freudian slip" helped spread his ideas about unconscious motivation to the general public. His views about sexuality and the significance of childhood were brought together in *Three Essays on the Theory of Sexuality* in 1905. This was a period of remarkable creativity, and the ideas in these books form the core of psychoanalysis. Although he continued to write and publish until close to the end of his life in 1939, his main theories, with a few exceptions, were all in place by 1905.

In 1902 Freud began to meet once a week with four other physicians at his apartment, and this "Wednesday Psychological Society" (expanded within a few years into the Vienna Psychoanalytic Society) was the beginning of psychoanalysis as an international movement. The early members of the group, who were all physicians, were Alfred Adler, Max Kahane, Rudolph Reitler, and Wilhelm Stekel. Over the next few years psychoanalysis spread beyond Vienna, and societies were established in Berlin, Budapest, London, New York, and Zurich. These groups, along with Freud's prolific publications, launched psychoanalysis as the most prominent form of psychological therapy.

Psychoanalysis as a "movement" or "cause," as Freud typically referred to it, became increasingly rigid. The same is true of his form of treatment. By the time he saw Ida/Dora in 1900, he was using the kind of therapy that he would practice for the rest of his life. The patient is instructed to free-associate, to say whatever comes to mind no matter how unimportant it may seem. The analyst looks for resistances and interprets or "clears them away," the repressed or unconscious material is then exposed, and its meaning is interpreted. The goal of the analysis is to make what was unconscious conscious, to put into words what had before been expressed through symptoms. Breuer's stress on emotional expression (catharsis) was largely replaced by the search for intellectual insight.

Several sources show how Freud practiced as a therapist. His six published case studies have been taught for years in psychoanalytic institutes as examples of the master at work: Dora (1905), Little Hans (1909), The Rat Man (1909), Judge Schreber (1911), The Wolf Man (1918), and The Young Homosexual Woman (1920). There are also several book-length accounts written by patients themselves—Joseph Wortis (1954), the poet H. D. (1956), Smiley Blanton (1971), John Dorsey (1976), and Abram Kardiner (1977)—as well as interviews with former patients conducted by the historian Paul Roazen and other investigators.

Psychoanalysis as a form of treatment is the starting place for almost all modern methods of psychotherapy, which have been elaborated in many directions, many completely at odds with the way Freud practiced. Nevertheless, they all begin with Freud and the treatment he developed as he gave up hypnotic suggestion and the pressure technique. One sees intimations of his new approach in the case of Ilona Weiss, in which, while still using suggestion, he let her tell her story in her own way. When Freud wrote about his cases, they came alive as unique individuals who lived in families and had their own childhood experiences. This may seem obvious now, but it is not the way most doctors wrote about their patients at that time, when they were not even given names but just seen as so many "hysterics" or "neurasthenics."

At its best, psychoanalytic therapy allows patients to tell their life stories in their own words, to reveal things they have hidden out of politeness, guilt, shame, or the conviction that no one would be interested. The patients with whom Freud was most successful commented on his intense concentration on what they said, his interest in understanding them, and the relief they experienced when an interpretation revealed an aspect of themselves they were not aware of. He was able to do this with individuals who were relatively compliant, venerated his authority, and with whom he could identify. Ironically, his therapeutic flaws and failures were most in evidence in his published cases, because with them he was often trying to promote his theories or prove the superiority of his approach.

The American psychiatrist Abram Kardiner, who saw Freud for six months in 1921, is an example of a successful psychoanalytic treatment; he later wrote a book about his experience that shows Freud at his therapeutic best. Kardiner had an extremely traumatic early life, growing up in poverty with a violent father and a mother who had tuberculosis. After describing the misery of his earliest years to Freud in his first session, "The Professor" told him he had made "a perfect presentation." Kardiner's mother died when he was three, and he spent most of the day alone in the family apartment with her body. All his life he had suffered from a phobia of masks and wax figures that mystified him. When Freud told him, "The first mask you saw was your dead mother's face," it was so revealing that Kardiner shivered with recognition. The interpretation also confirmed his belief in Freud's powers of insight.

A few years after his mother's death, Kardiner's father remarried, and his new stepmother took the young boy into her bed and had him fondle her breasts. Although gratifying, this also left him feeling guilty and afraid of his father. This was ripe material for Freud's Oedipal interpretation, which alleviated his patient's fear and guilt, though what Kardiner had experienced was a real seduction and not a fantasy.

Freud clearly liked Kardiner and conveyed this in his praise. Unlike his largely silent treatment of other patients seen at the same time, with this traumatized young man he was relatively talkative. The overall experience was very helpful, but Kardiner also noted that Freud's interpretation of his "unconscious homosexuality" put him "on a wild-goose chase for years for a problem that did not exist." Although the interpretation of the mask phobia shows Freud identifying with this man who, like himself as a young boy, lived in poverty and had suffered maternal loss, the interpretation of unconscious homosexuality came from theory and had nothing to do with Kardiner's life, though it reflected Freud's own concern with what he once referred to as his "unruly homosexual libido." To put it another way, to make the interpretation of the mask phobia, Freud had to imagine himself as a very young, frightened child, left with a waxy-faced dead mother. His interpretation of unconscious homosexuality, on the other hand, was based not on such empathy, but on a theory that came from his uncertainty about his own masculinity.

Freud's analysis of Ida Bauer ("Dora") stands in sharp contrast to Kardiner's largely successful treatment. An adolescent girl, she was brought to him by her wealthy father and suffered from a variety of symptoms:

headaches, shortness of breath, a nervous cough, and depression with suicidal impulses. Freud interpreted all these symptoms, as well as her
dreams, as expressions of conflict over her unconscious Oedipal-sexual
wishes. When his patient did not agree with him, he interpreted this as her
resistance. The case contains scant evidence to support Freud's interpretations, though he relentlessly forced them on the young girl. In reality, her
father was lying to her about an affair he was having with a woman, for-
merly Ida's friend and confidant, whose husband, an older man, tried to seduce Ida when she was thirteen years old. In addition, her mother was
unavailable because of her frenzied house cleaning, which drove everyone
in the family crazy. All these factors played significant roles in the development of Ida's symptoms, but most of all the attempted sexual molestation
and the obfuscations used to cover it up. Freud had to admit that the case
was not a success, but he did not modify his Oedipal theory.

At the same time, it was out of this botched treatment that he expanded one of his most original and important concepts, already hinted at
in *Studies*: transference. Transference is the manifestation of past relationships in the patient's way of relating to the therapist. Freud later added the
concept of countertransference, the analyst's unconscious reactions toward
the patient.

Freud codified the technique of what came to be called classical psychoanalysis in six papers written between 1911 and 1915 when his stature was established. They laid out the rules analysts were obliged to follow. Patients
should be seen for a fixed number of hours—originally six per week, later
shortened to five—and were required to pay a set fee whether they came to
their sessions or not. They lay on the couch with the analyst sitting behind,
a practice begun by Freud because, he said, "I cannot put up with being
stared at by other people for eight hours a day." Analysts should maintain
their "anonymity," revealing nothing about themselves; the treatment
should be carried out "under privation, in a state of abstinence"; and they
should follow the rule of "neutrality," that is, an analyst should behave
"like a surgeon who puts aside all his feelings, even his human sympathy,
and concentrates his mental forces on the single aim of performing the
operation as skillfully as possible."

When Freud followed these rules (which he often did not), his patients did not make much progress. His well-known published cases are failures, such as Ida Bauer and the "Young Homosexual Woman," or at best partial successes, such as the "Rat Man" and the "Wolf Man." In contrast are patients like Kardiner and others—cases he never wrote or publicly spoke about—all of whom found their analyses very helpful. With these patients, what was curative was not neutrality, anonymity, abstinence, or interpretations of resistance, but a more open and supportive relationship, interpretations that fit their unique experiences, empathy, praise, and the feeling that they were liked by their analyst, whose view of them, because he was the famous Sigmund Freud, had an enormous impact. Because he only publicly advocated the classical technique, it came to define the way analysts practiced for many years, even though in a great number of cases it was unhelpful, if not harmful, to patients.

Another of Freud's important contributions is found in *The Interpretation of Dreams,* which he always considered his most significant book. *Interpretation* is filled with provocative ideas, new ways of understanding the half-hidden world of fantasy and imagination. Using his own dreams and those of many others, he is persuasive in showing how dreams have meaning and are related to the events of daily life, including the lives of ordinary people. He demonstrates that everyone has an active unconscious, not just hysterics or neurotics. Dreams are stimulated by "day residues"— emotion-laden events from the pre-sleep period—and transform these into a private "language" of visual symbols. His interpretations translate these pictorial dramas back into understandable terms. Using a great number of examples, he made dreams part of normal life, including familiar dreams of being embarrassed in public, feeling anxious before an examination or performance, or feeling "rooted to the spot," unable to move in the face of danger.

Then there are the familiar Freudian symbols: sticks, daggers, guns, and the like, which stand for the penis, and boxes, chests, cupboards, ovens, and other enclosed spaces, which represent the female genitalia. Walking up and down steps, ladders, or staircases was thought to symbolize sexual intercourse. Freud was of two minds about the universal nature of such symbols. At one point in *Interpretation* he cautioned against using such symbols as if they were figures in a codebook with fixed meanings. One must get each dreamer's associations and interpret the dream in its individual context. But at another point his need for a universal theory led him to state, "Symbols allow us in certain circumstances to interpret a dream without questioning the dreamer, who indeed would in any case have nothing to tell us about the symbol."

Freud's penchant for all-encompassing theories led him to pronounce that "all dreams are wish fulfillments," which he later modified to "a dream is the disguised fulfillment of a suppressed or repressed [sexual] wish." But the many dreams presented in his book do not support this assertion. They involve a variety of motives: wishes to have power, including children's dreams that symbolize their longing "to be big"; and attempts to make up for mistakes, alleviate feelings of guilt, come to terms with feelings of inadequacy, or deal with fears and anxieties. If interpreted with an understanding of each person's unique life and social context, dreams can be one, though not the only, "royal road to the unconscious."

Another of Freud's major contributions was his exposure of the hypocrisy and crippling sexual repressions of the Victorian age. Contradicting the myth of childhood innocence, he wrote about "infantile sexuality" and opened up the world of childhood sexual-emotional experience to exploration. *Three Essays on the Theory of Sexuality* exploded out of his earlier ideas about neurosis and sexuality in a variety of creative directions. These included new ways of seeing many sexual practices or "perversions"; hypotheses about the development of masculine and feminine identity; a theory of developmental stages (oral, anal, Oedipal, latency); and ideas about ambivalence, bisexuality, masochism, sadism, and related topics. The general effect of all these ideas was to help people feel less guilty and less isolated about what they had thought of as their own peculiar sexual feelings and fantasies. To take just one example, children today hardly experience the fear and self-reproaches about masturbation that they did in the nineteenth and early twentieth centuries. The same is gradually becoming true about homosexuality. The contrast between the old and new attitudes is striking.

Three Essays begins with a very balanced discussion of homosexuality. Freud noted that it was valued in the high civilization of ancient Athens and that a number of historical figures were homosexual. At other places, however, he described "homosexual libido" as a terrible danger to men and, in one of his final essays, *Analysis Terminable and Interminable* of 1937, he cited a man's "passive or feminine attitude to another male" as the strongest resistance to analytic cure. Such an attitude can certainly be seen in his own infatuation with Wilhelm Fliess, although the threat of homosexuality is not a universal experience, as the example of Kardiner shows. Freud's definition of homosexuality as a "perversion" that could be "cured" by psychoanalysis had deleterious effects for many years. It was not until 1974 that it was removed from the official manual of psychiatric disorders.

Freud's ideas about infantile sexuality, in some ways problematic, also contained the important theory of the way childhood emotional relations shape adult character. Why does a man fall in love with a certain type of woman? Why is one person sexually aroused by members of the opposite sex, another by undergarments, and a third by members of the same sex? Why are some individuals hypersexual, "Don Juans," or nymphomaniacs, and others relatively unresponsive? The answers to such questions, Freud argued, were to be found in the person's history, in childhood experiences, of which the adult practices and preferences were the end result. Put another way, one's early relationships establish patterns—images, fantasies, emotional predispositions, and expectations—that determine adult feelings and choices. As Freud put it,

> It often happens that a young man falls in love . . . with a mature woman, or a girl with an elderly man in a position of authority; this is clearly an echo of the phase of development that we have been discussing, since these figures are able to re-animate pictures of their mother or father. There can be no doubt that every object-choice whatever is based, though less closely, on these prototypes. . . . In view of the importance of a child's relations to his parents in determining his later choice of a sexual object, it can easily be understood

that any disturbance of those relations will produce the gravest effects upon his adult sexual life.

The theory of childhood prototypes has passed into the common domain. We take it for granted that the experiences of our early years influence who we are and the form of our later relationships: how we love and
hate, sexual preferences, choice of partners, and much more. But these
ideas did not exist before Freud. There was some recognition that "the
child is father to the man," but when it came to the specifics, pre-Freudian
writers spoke of general factors such as "inheritance" or family history—
that is, whether members of earlier generations were alcoholic, violent,
feeble-minded, or insane. Freud was only partly right about some of the
specific ways in which childhood experience shapes adult personality, but
his general model has had an enormous influence. We routinely trace a
number of psychological problems to family experiences: a rejecting or
overly critical mother, an alcoholic or abusive father, parents who were too
demanding or who lacked loving connections with their children.

A similar mixture of valuable insights and personal blind spots charac-
terizes many of the other topics discussed in *Three Essays*, particularly
Freud's well-known theory of the psychosexual stages of development. He
describes the first stage of development as "oral," which captures, in a very
important way, the infant's pre-language, bodily-emotional way of encoun-
tering the world. Babies do relate to their environment by sucking, but they
also do so by looking, touching, clinging, and, of greatest significance,
forming a powerful attachment to their mother or other primary caretaker.
Freud's neglect of the importance of attachments is a major failing, not
just in *Three Essays*, but throughout his theories. His avoidance of the centrality of attachment is the most pernicious effect of his failure to come to
terms with his own history of traumatic losses.

Freud's concept of the "anal" stage is also flawed because he focused on
the pleasures and frustrations of the anal "erotogenic zone." This stage,
known to parents as "the terrible twos," would have been better characterized as the battleground that pits the young child's emerging autonomy
against adult authority. Still, if one uses Freud's idea of prototypes here,

one can understand later relations with authority figures—rebelliousness or over-submissiveness, for example—as the adult outcomes of the experiences of this age.

Freud's theory of the Oedipus complex, which he viewed as a great discovery and the core of everyone's neurosis, is most problematic. As he described it in a footnote added to *Three Essays* in 1920,

> It has justly been said that the Oedipus complex is the nuclear complex of the neuroses, and constitutes the essential part of their content. It represents the peak of infantile sexuality, which, through its after-effects, exercises a decisive influence on the sexuality of adults. Every new arrival on this planet is faced by the task of mastering the Oedipus complex; anyone who fails to do so falls a victim to neurosis. With the progress of psychoanalytic studies the importance of the Oedipus complex has become more and more clearly evident; its recognition has become the shibboleth that distinguishes the adherents of psychoanalysis from its opponents.

Note the grand sweep of this theory: It covers "every new arrival on this planet," regardless of genetic background, temperament, culture, family, or social circumstances. Acceptance of the Oedipus complex did become the psychoanalytic "shibboleth," an Old Testament term meaning a test that separates religious believers from heretics. Failure to accept the ubiquitous nature of sexual motivation and the Oedipus complex was central to the disagreements with all the major figures who broke with Freud, including Alfred Adler, Wilhelm Stekel, C. G. Jung, and many others. Later evidence has shown that they were right and Freud wrong; it simply isn't true that the Oedipus complex is "the nuclear complex" of every neurosis. In fact, in the way Freud defined it, as a conflict between the child's sexual fantasies and reality, it isn't much of a factor in anyone's neurosis. *

Although it is easy for parents to observe Oedipal reactions in their children—"Why doesn't Daddy go away so I can sleep with you, Mommy?"—such feelings are not the source of great conflicts, and children typically outgrow them. The Oedipal situation becomes a locus of psychological trouble only when inappropriate acts are initiated by a parent: the lonely woman who takes her son into bed with her and sexualizes the relationship, the predatory father who molests his daughter or, as in the case of Ida Bauer, hands her over to the husband of his mistress as a quid pro quo—you close your eyes to the sexual affair I am having with your wife and I won't look at your attempts to seduce my daughter. When there are Oedipal problems it is because real things have been done to the child.

The idea of the boy's sexual attraction to his mother and rivalry with his father first occurred to Freud in his self-analysis, and he later expanded the theory in several ways. The young boy (Oedipal theory always fit boys more than girls) who observed that his mother or sisters do not have penises imagined that he would be castrated by his father as punishment for his sexual desire for his mother. "Castration anxiety" then became the primary source of all other forms of neurotic fear. According to Freud, the "healthy" or non-neurotic resolution of the conflict is to accept the father's superior power and identify with him. This identification then becomes the basis for the "superego" or conscience, defined as an inner father or authority that makes one feel guilty for disobedience. The Oedipal theory thus explained two of the most prominent features seen in patients: anxiety (defined as the fear of castration) and the self-reproaches that were so prominent in many of the cases in *Studies* and are still found in a great many patients. Again, the theory posits fantasies rather than reality as the foundation of neurotic anxiety and problems with a punitive conscience. In fact, boys during Freud's day were routinely threatened with castration if they masturbated or engaged in sexual play, and some girls had their clitorises surgically removed to prevent masturbation, which was viewed as a dangerous practice. Castration was no fantasy but an actual threat, frequently accompanied by punishment for sexual "misbehavior."

Anxiety is a prominent symptom found in almost all neurotic patients, from the women in *Studies* to the present. It is also an emotion that Freud himself experienced, as early as the fear of train travel that appeared at age three. His earliest views, drawing on widespread medical and quasi-medical ideas of the nineteenth century, tied it to sexuality. In these speculations, he thought anxiety was a consequence of blocked or improperly discharged sexual energy. With the full development of his theory of the Oedipus complex, however, castration anxiety moved to center stage; for many years it was seen as the basis for all other manifestations of this disruptive emotion.

Identification has proven to be a very useful concept, but it is a much more straightforward process than that outlined by Freud in his Oedipal theory. Children imitate and model themselves after their parents, older siblings, and other figures, not out of fear of castration, but because of love and admiration, wishes to be bigger and more powerful, or as a result of direct rewards and punishments. The same is true for the development of a severe or punitive conscience. It is a consequence of how the child is actually treated: whether rules are enforced harshly or with kindness, whether parents withdraw their love when the child misbehaves or are attuned to his or her emotional needs.

It is one of the tragedies of psychoanalysis that Freud insisted on the centrality of the Oedipus complex despite the lack of supporting evidence, thus marring work filled with many insights and provocative new ideas. Of course he thought that had found such evidence in his cases, but an examination reveals that most of the "evidence" consisted of speculative interpretations that his patients had to comply with; when they did not, they were accused of "resistance," rejected, or subjected to his hostility. Perhaps his insistence on the centrality of this theory was inevitable because the idea of a "universal" Oedipus complex—a law that would make him a great scientist—first came to him at the point in his self-analysis when he was confronted with his childhood traumas. It served a defensive function that grew stronger with the passage of time.

There was one significant exception to Freud's tracing of the core of everyone's neurosis to the Oedipus complex and castration anxiety: the revisions he proposed in *Inhibitions, Symptoms, and Anxiety* (1926). In this work, written in reaction to Otto Rank's *The Trauma of Birth* (1924), Freud made a striking about-face. After a certain amount of vacillation, he was able to state that his earlier ideas were wrong, something he rarely did, and to outline a new theory. Anxiety is a "signal" of "danger," the danger of the recurrence of a "trauma," the trauma being the "loss of the love object or its love." Freud wrote that,

> It was anxiety which produced repression and not, as I formerly believed, repression which produced anxiety. . . . It is always the ego's attitude of anxiety which is the primary thing and which sets repression going. Anxiety never arises from repressed libido. . . . Anxiety arose originally as a reaction to a state of danger and it is reproduced whenever a state of that kind recurs . . . [such as] when the child is alone, or in the dark, or when it finds itself with an unknown person instead of one to whom it is used—such as its mother. These three instances can be reduced to a single condition—namely, that of missing someone who is loved and longed for.

In the discussion that followed, Freud stressed the "infant's mental helplessness," which was "conditioned by separation from the mother." His new ideas about anxiety contained three crucial changes. He moved anxiety into its proper place as a major cause of symptoms. For example, if one has "blocked" sexuality, it is because one is anxious about sexual performance, not the other way around. Next, he returned to Breuer's recognition of the importance of trauma, and, more broadly, to the significance of real events in the causation of neuroses. And finally, he recognized the great importance of the mother and the child's attachment to her. It should be obvious that in this essay he is finally able to address (albeit in general theoretical terms) the traumatic origins of his own anxiety. It is also true that, despite the revolutionary ideas expressed in this essay, in his subsequent work Freud seems to have forgotten that he wrote it. The insights about anxiety, trauma, and the child's need for mothering rarely appeared in his subsequent writings, in which he returned to Oedipus, castration anxiety, and the importance of the father. Nevertheless, the 1926 essay was the starting point for contemporary investigators of maternal attachment and separation, beginning with the work of John Bowlby.

Psychoanalysis might have been integrated into universities, with their traditions of scholarship and tolerance for different theories and points of view. But Freud always claimed that he was unappreciated by the academic world and was determined to found his own, independent organization. The group that began meeting in 1902 brought together intelligent, creative men, physicians and others, who were interested in his exciting new ideas. In the beginning there were open discussions and the presentations of papers that expanded on one or another psychoanalytic topic, but as the musicologist Max Graf, an early member of the society and the father of the boy who became the case of "Little Hans," noted,

> The last and decisive word was always spoken by Freud himself. There was an atmosphere of the foundation of a religion in that room. Freud himself was its prophet who made the heretofore prevailing methods of psychological investigation appear superficial. . . . Freud's pupils—he was always addressed [as] "The Professor"— were his apostles.

The pattern set in these meetings prevailed throughout the history of psychoanalysis. Freud liked to speak of it as a "science," but psychoanalysis had more in common with religions, political movements, or cults. Nowhere was this more apparent than in the treatment of members who presented new ideas or raised questions about Freud's shibboleths. They were routinely attacked as "anti-sexual," suffering from "resistance," a threat to the hard-won insights of psychoanalysis, and were expelled from the group. Freud was even more vitriolic in his private correspondence, labeling those who disagreed with him as driven by "boundless ambition," "neurotic," "perverse," or "crazy."

Josef Breuer was the first of Freud's collaborators to be rejected when he failed to completely agree with his colleague's ideas; not just rejected, but made the object of a false story that depicted him as a coward. Alfred Adler suffered the fate of expulsion when he presented his creative ideas and was forced out of the group in 1911, along with Freud's first follower, Wilhelm Stekel. Sensing that more "deviations" were in the offing, the most loyal followers—Ernest Jones, Karl Abraham, and a few others— formed a group called "The Committee," whose purpose was to protect

The Professor and his theories. Jung, who like Adler was working on his own ideas, was the next to be excommunicated, in 1913. And so it went over the years: Otto Rank was dropped in 1924 and Sandor Ferenczi in 1932, in spite of the significant value of their contributions, their deep involvement in and support of psychoanalysis for many years, and their close personal ties to Freud. Those who disagreed with orthodox doctrines or came up with new ideas were blacklisted, not given referrals—which Freud largely controlled—and their reputations were tarnished with lies and slander. The fate of these "dissidents" was an object lesson to those who wished to remain within the movement: This was what would happen if they dared to raise questions about Freud and his doctrines.

Freud's childhood identification with heroic military leaders was crucial to the way he shaped the movement. He envisioned himself as the commander of a psychoanalytic army that was surrounded by enemies, against whom he and his loyal lieutenants must battle. How different things would have been if, instead of a cult-like "cause," psychoanalysis had really been the science that it claimed to be, a field in which new ideas and methods were examined, tested against observations, and welcomed when they proved fruitful in producing further research and more effective therapy. But this was not to be. Freud made some significant additions and corrections—the revision of the theory of anxiety in *Inhibitions*, a new conception of the effects of trauma, repetitive traumatic dreams, and a drive toward mastery in the opening chapters of *Beyond the Pleasure Principle*—but the contributions of others who remained as loyal followers were slavish reworkings of his ideas. Almost all significant new developments in both theory and therapy came from those who worked outside the psychoanalytic mainstream: Adler, Jung, Rank, Ferenczi, the neo-Freudians (Karen Horney, Erich Fromm, Harry Stack Sullivan, Erik Erikson), and, more recently, John Bowlby, Heinz Kohut, and relational and intersubjective theorists.

⸺

Freud's creations brought about profound changes in the way we view ourselves. At the same time, his significant and lasting contributions were mixed with invalid and at times destructive theories and practices. It is clear how Freud's drive to create a large-scale theory created difficulties. At the same time, his interrelated system of concepts enhanced his influence and helped spread liberating ideas. Take, for example, that most central concept, the unconscious. Many philosophers and writers, Arthur Schopenhauer and Friedrich Nietzsche among them, had had the idea, but it was Breuer who first used it to understand and treat hysteria, and Freud who embedded it in a theory that applied to neuroses, dreams, childhood events, and the slips and errors of everyday life, thus giving it a depth missing from earlier accounts. Freud did not invent the concept of the unconscious, but he defined and used it in a way that made it broadly meaningful and useful.

Despite his many creative and liberating contributions, a number of Freud's ideas were harmful and destructive. Most important is his neglect of the role of trauma and, more broadly, real events, in the creation of anxiety, guilt, shame, and psychological symptoms. Freud's insistence that sexual conflicts and fantasies were primary causes goes back to his break with Breuer in the 1890s. Although he occasionally gave credit to real traumas, as in *Beyond the Pleasure Principle* and *Inhibitions, Symptoms, and Anxiety,* this was never his dominant position, nor that of his loyal followers. Nowhere was this more striking than in his appraisal of the effects of World War I on the soldiers trapped in that horror. A great many of them could be found in the streets of Vienna after the war, showing the signs of what was then called "shell shock," with symptoms much like those of the hysterics he had treated in the 1890s. He must have seen many of them every day when he took his regular afternoon walk.

Without having treated a single survivor of the war, Freud proclaimed, "It is, however, a significant fact that, when war conditions ceased to operate, the greater number of the neurotic disturbances brought about by the war simultaneously vanished." Partly due to his influence, it took another fifty years for the extremely long-lasting effects of such traumas, now called PTSD or post-traumatic stress disorder, to be recognized. Along with his dismissal of the traumas of war went a neglect of adult trauma more generally. His recognition of the importance of early childhood was a valuable contribution, but by making it the exclusive determinant of adult personality, Freud neglected the effects of all experiences after the first years of life: adolescent struggles, midlife crises, and the difficulties associated with aging and death.

Freud's retrograde ideas about women never changed from the time of his engagement to Martha, when he espoused the widespread idea that women should not strive for equality with men. Breuer, in his treatment of Bertha Pappenheim, made clear that the limitations imposed on her because she was a woman were a significant cause of her breakdown. Later, a number of investigators—such as the widely read sex researcher Havelock Ellis—changed their ideas about women in response to new evidence and the feminist movement. Freud, in contrast, simply poured his old prejudices into new psychoanalytic bottles. In place of ideas about inherent inferiority, he claimed that all women suffered from "penis envy," which presumably began in childhood when they discovered they did not possess the organ that their father or brothers had. In Freud's theory, this became the most significant event in their development. The "healthy" resolution was to recognize the fact that they would never have a penis and accept the limited role of wife and mother as their rightful place. A baby would be the substitute for what they were missing.

For many years Freudian analysts told women that their healthy strivings—for higher education, greater independence, a career in which their talents could be expressed—were symptoms of their neurotic penis envy. If the Oedipus complex defined the conflict that every boy "on the planet" must come to terms with, according to this theory every woman, whatever her intelligence, temperament, or creative abilities, should follow the single path of marriage and motherhood.

Freud's neglect of the importance of society was another deficiency in his thinking. Because of his need for a universal theory, he had almost nothing to say about cultural or social differences; everyone in the world was driven by the same motives and beset by the same conflicts. At the core of this neglect was his theory of human instincts as non- or antisocial, his view that we are, from the beginning of life, driven by self-centered pleasure seeking. This instinct theory missed what has since been amply proven to be the powerful motive of attachment, the intrinsic need for social bonds. Freud's neglect of cultural factors also led him to ignore the effects of many social phenomena such as racial, religious, economic, and class discrimination, some of which had played a large role in his own life. After all, he did start out as a poor Jew in anti-Semitic Vienna. The cultural anthropology that he relied on in such books as *Totem and Taboo* and *Moses and Monotheism* had little scientific credibility. Social instincts were brought back into the field by John Bowlby and the many investigators who continued his research with the theories of attachment and separation anxiety, and other social-cultural factors have been explored in the works of such neo-Freudians as Karen Horney, Erik Erikson, and Erich Fromm.

The baleful effects of shaping psychoanalysis as a cult-like movement or cause grew out of Freud's need to be a great man; it was the basis of all the other problems with his theories and approaches to therapy. For many years treatment was frozen in the classical mold of anonymity, abstinence, neutrality, the fifty-minute hour, and the silent analyst sitting out of view, all of which Freud defined as "the pure gold" of analysis, in contrast to the "base metal" of other forms of treatment. It didn't matter that his own cases provided little solid evidence for the success of treatments based on this technique, or that countless patients spent years "on the couch" with little effect. Theory within the classical establishment fared no better; Freud's texts were treated as holy writ, every word subjected to endless exegesis.

Reactions to Freud tend to be polarized. On the one hand, he is idolized, and those who dare to raise questions are labeled "Freud bashers," whether their criticisms are measured and well founded or not. On the other hand, his work, if not all of psychotherapy, is dismissed as fakery because some of his ideas were wrong. Such extreme reactions are out of place. Pointing out where Freud was in error is not "bashing" but the kind of evaluation that is necessary to develop more valid approaches. And dismissing all of psychotherapy because a number of his ideas were false does not help in the development of theories and treatment methods that can be vital to those who struggle with psychological difficulties.

For all its flaws, Freud's creation of psychoanalysis as a large explanatory system was a great achievement. He opened up many heretofore neglected areas and developed new ways of thinking about human psychology and treating patients. The theories and techniques that were misguided have been criticized, revised, and corrected by later investigators and therapists.

The "classical" psychoanalysis that Freud created lives on in an ever-dwindling number of psychoanalytic institutes, as well as in the minds of a small number of the faithful. The understanding of psychological disturbance and its treatment has moved on. Work in the last thirty to forty years reveals that, in large measure, Breuer's ideas were more valid than Freud's. A collaborative relationship between therapist and patient—one that involves empathy and active support—is much more helpful than the neutral, abstinent, all-knowing stance of the orthodox psychoanalyst. The full expression of strangulated emotions is crucial for healing, along with insight and understanding. Sexual conflicts are prominent in certain individuals, but are not the only cause of neuroses. In the case of Bertha Pappenheim, Breuer recognized discrimination against women as one cause of her breakdown. He made clear that traumas and other real experiences were sources of psychological suffering and that dissociation was a common means of coping with them, in contrast to Freud's fixation on sexual drives, fantasies, and repression.

Breuer envisioned a field of critical inquiry rather than a doctrinaire movement. He advocated tolerance for a variety of theories and treatment methods, in contrast to Freud's "shibboleths," "iron clad" laws, and "pure gold." If the discoveries in *Studies* had developed along the path Breuer sketched out, psychoanalysis and related forms of psychotherapy would have been spared many of their most problematic features. This development has finally occurred in the last few decades, which have witnessed a return to a scientific approach consistent with Breuer's work. He would have welcomed the research on infancy, child development, trauma, women's studies, and psychotherapy that has played its part in overthrowing Freud's doctrines. We have come full circle and returned to many of the rich possibilities that were first outlined by Breuer in the *Studies on Hysteria.*

ACKNOWLEDGMENTS

I express my deepest appreciation to my wife Barbara: first reader, perceptive critic, and source of the title of the book and the chapter names. She also discovered the epigraphs that begin each chapter. My thanks to my agent and friend, John W. Wright, for his faith in me; he, along with Amanda Moon at Basic Books, was crucial in bringing this project into existence. Amanda and her assistant, Whitney Casser, have been a pleasure to work with, and the book has benefited from Amanda's careful and thorough editing and the copyediting of Sharon DeJohn. I have been blessed with another reader, my friend and colleague, Professor Bernard J. Paris, who gave most generously of his time and literary and editorial skills. I also want to express my thanks to Rebecca Newberger Goldstein for the quotation from William James that heads Chapter Two.

Several friends and colleagues read the book in manuscript form and made helpful suggestions as well as offering their support: Suzanne Gassner, David Markel, Tom Rosbrow, and Jim Lieberman. Jim also found seven letters in the Library of Congress Archives, never before available, written by Freud and Breuer in 1907–1908. I thank him for that, and Marianne Nemeth for translating the letters from German to English.

I wish to thank the following for permission to reprint copyrighted materials:

Extracts from *The Standard Edition of the Complete Psychological Works of Sigmund Freud*, all rights reserved, reproduced by arrangement with Paterson Marsh Ltd., London.

Extracts from *The Complete Letters of Sigmund Freud to Wilhelm Fliess*, © 1975 Sigmund Freud Copyrights Ltd. and J. M. Masson, reproduced by arrangement with Paterson Marsh Ltd., London.

NOTES

A more extensive version of the material covered in this book can be found in my biography *Freud: Darkness in the Midst of Vision* (2000), which also contains additional references and more extensive discussions.

CHAPTER ONE: EXPLORING THE IRRATIONAL

1 *If it is a merit:* Freud, *Five Lectures on Psychoanalysis,* 9.

3 *traced to the "anal" stage:* See Freud, *Some Character Types Met with in Psychoanalytic Work,* 1916.

CHAPTER TWO: THE VISION OF A HEROIC SELF

One of Freud's lasting contributions was the theory that adult character, relationships, and symptoms can be understood as disguised expressions of the emotional patterns laid down in childhood. In his own case, he recovered important memories from his earliest years during the self-analysis he carried out in his late thirties; this chapter draws on the information to be found there.

6 *The child grudges:* Freud "Femininity," *New Introductory Lectures,* 122.

6 *A mother is only:* Freud, "Femininity," *New Introductory Lectures,* 133.

6 *Further painful losses:* The interpretation of the great importance of Freud's early losses is spelled out in Breger, *Freud.* Atwood and Stolorow called attention to the way Freud's reactions to the loss of his mother are expressed in the *Femininity* essay in the chapter "Freud," in *Faces in a Cloud.* The interpretation is controversial and not shared by several biographers, among them Peter Gay in *Freud: A Life for Our Time,* though I believe the evidence is quite convincing, as well as being consistent with much recent work on attachment and loss, starting with

Bowlby in *Attachment and Loss*. See Wallin, *Attachment in Psychotherapy*, for a summary of research on attachment.

7   *souls, burning in hell:* For Freud's own account of this period, see Masson, *Complete Letters*, 268–272.

7   *I know from my youth:* Ibid., 374.

8   *The boy . . . cannot:* Freud, *Some Reflections on Schoolboy Psychology*, 241.

8   *I used to find:* Ibid., 241.

8   *Vienna office were filled:* Pictures of the artifacts in Freud's office can be found in Engelman, *Bergasse 19*.

9   *lasted all his life:* In the last years of his life, when Freud was escaping the Nazis, he imagined himself as William the Conqueror, arriving in England.

9   *friends as "study mates":* Berneys, "My Brother Sigmund Freud," 142.

9   *highly emotional, easily:* M. Freud, *Sigmund Freud*, 11.

10   *shrill and domineering:* Heller, "Freud's Mother and Father," 335–339.

11   *a school of scientific:* Ellenberger, *Discovery of the Unconscious*, 474.

11   *in Brücke's physiological:* This and the earlier quotations about Brücke are taken from Freud, *Autobiographical Study*, 9–10.

13   *awoke in tears:* Freud, *Interpretation of Dreams*, 584.

13   *his darling "Marty":* The fraction of Freud's letters to Martha that have been made public can be found in E. L. Freud, *Letters of Sigmund Freud*.

14   *how not being:* quoted in Clark, *Freud*, 89.

14   *It seems a completely:* Ibid., 76.

14   *unmarried sister Minna:* Peter Swales has argued in "Freud, Minna Bernays, and the Conquest of Rome" that Freud had an affair with his sister-in-law Minna, a story that originated with some remarks made by Jung when he visited Freud in 1907. Swales develops a complicated theory, reinterpreting some of Freud's slips and dreams, in which he places Freud and Minna in an Italian spa together and concludes that they had an affair from which Minna became pregnant, with Freud eventually paying for an abortion. It has recently been revealed that they did register together at that spa at the time Swales claims. The story depends on a number of guesses and suppositions about events that may or may not have occurred and that cannot be verified. I think an affair would have been completely out of character for both of them, who were, to put it mildly, very emotionally constricted individuals. In addition, Freud was more attracted to men than to women (what he referred to as his "unruly homosexual libido"), though there is no evidence that any of his relationships (with

Fleischl, Fliess, Jung) passed beyond intellectual infatuations. But the main point, in my view, is what difference would it make if Freud and Minna did have an affair? It would change nothing about the truth or lack of truth of his theories or the effectiveness of his therapy. Jung and Ferenczi did have affairs, but this tells us nothing about whether their theories were valid or their treatment methods effective.

14   *I must admit:* Martha Freud, quoted in Laforgue, "Personal Memories of Sigmund Freud," 342.

15   *This brings us to:* Freud, *"Civilized" Sexual Morality and Modern Nervous Illness,* 194–195.

16   *Sexual excitement, too:* Freud to Fliess, Masson, *Complete Letters,* 54.

16   *My Indian summer:* Freud, in McGuire, *Freud/Jung letters,* 292.

16   *I stand for an:* E. L. Freud, *Letters of Sigmund Freud,* 308.

16   *I always think:* Freud to Martha, quoted in Jones, *Life and Work,* 140.

17   *the pained expression:* Ibid., 17–18.

17   *The mob gives:* Freud to Martha, in E. L. Freud, *Letters of Sigmund Freud,* 50.

17   *not a bad solution:* quoted in Appignanesi and Forrester, *Freud's Women,* 42.

18   *There is ample:* Jones, *Life and Work,* 304–305.

18   *experimenting with cocaine:* A full account of Freud's involvement with cocaine can be found in Byck, *Cocaine Papers by Sigmund Freud.*

19   *I admire and:* Freud to Martha, quoted in Jones, *Life and Work,* 90.

19   *I ask myself:* Ibid., 91.

CHAPTER THREE: A SCIENTIST TREATS THE PASSIONS

A complete account of Josef Breuer's life and work can be found in the excellent biography by Albrecht Hirschmüller, *The Life and Work of Josef Breuer* (published in German in 1978; English translation, 1989).

22   *Neither at that time:* Freud, *Autobiographical Study,* 8.

22   *I have no great:* Kardiner, *My Analysis with Freud,* 68–69.

23   *on the whole:* Hirschmüller, *Life and Work of Josef Breuer,* 13.

24   *stalwart critic of:* Ibid., 49.

25   *a monthly stipend:* The letters obtained by Jim Lieberman from the Library of Congress show Freud trying to repay the money in 1907, although Breuer didn't think he was owed anything.

25   *like sitting in the sun:* Freud to Martha, quoted in Jones, *Life and Work,* 167.

CHAPTER FOUR: THE TALKING CURE:
JOSEF BREUER AND ANNA O.

A great deal has been written about the case of Anna O. See: Appignanesi and Forrester, *Freud's Women*; Borch-Jacobson, *Remembering Anna O.*; Ellenberger, "The Story of Anna O."; Freeman, *The Story of Anna O.*; Rosenbaum and Muroff, *Anna O.*; and Swenson, "Freud's 'Anna O.'."

29   *a friend of Martha:* Appignanesi and Forrester, *Freud's Women*, 81.

30   *pseudonym Anna O.:* The identity of "Anna O." was first revealed by Ernest Jones in *Life and Work*.

30   *having two selves:* Freud (with Breuer), *Studies on Hysteria*, 24.

30   *excessive but quite:* Ibid., 24.

31   *His commitment to:* Hirschmüller, *Life and Work of Josef Breuer*, 129.

31   *life became known:* Freud (with Breuer), *Studies*, 21–22.

32   *producing those countless:* Hirschmüller, *Life and Work of Josef Breuer*, 100.

32   *She was markedly:* Freud (with Breuer), *Studies*, 21.

33   *The sexual element:* Breuer's original notes, in Hirschmüller, *Life and Work of Josef Breuer*, 277–278.

33   *an object of:* Ibid., 277.

33   *This girl, who:* Freud (with Breuer), *Studies*, 22.

34   *she was completely:* Ibid., 21.

34   *her little dog:* Ibid., 34–35.

35   *Her right arm:* Ibid., 38–39.

36   *for two weeks:* Ibid., 25.

36   *stated in the article:* Although "Preliminary Communication" was coauthored, the case of Anna O. is entirely Breuer's work.

36   *each individual hysterical:* Ibid., 6.

37   *Hysterics suffer mainly:* Ibid., 7.

37   *the First World War:* See chapter 18 in Breger, *Freud*, for a discussion of the neuroses of war and their similarity to the symptoms found in "hysteria."

38   *to turn the head:* Martha to Freud, Appignanesi and Forrester, *Freud's Women*, 488.

39   *She was moreover:* Freud (with Breuer), *Studies*, 41.

40   *We now know:* Information about the later life of Bertha Pappenheim can be found in Ellenberger, *Discovery of the Unconscious*, and Hirschmüller, *Life and Work of Josef Breuer*.

40   *I hope that my patient:* Breuer, quoted in Hirschmüller, *Life and Work of Josef Breuer*, 294.

40   *A mood of unrelieved:* See Hirschmüller, *Life and Work of Josef Breuer,* 121–125 for a detailed account of Bertha's early writings. A book of her early stories, all quite charming and well written, has recently been issued in an English translation; see Pappenheim, *In the Junk Shop.*

41   *I have come to:* Freud, *On the History,* 8.

41   *Now I have strong:* Freud, *On the History,* 12.

42   *been endlessly recycled:* Despite access to information supplied by Ellenberger in "The Story of Anna O.," and Hirschmüller, *Life and Times of Josef Breuer,* Peter Gay perpetuates the myth in *Freud: A Life for Our Time.*

42   *this immersion in:* Breuer, quoted in Cranefield, "Josef Breuer's Evaluation," 320.

43   *The main contribution:* Ibid., 321.

44   *This account fits with:* The most extensive account can be found in Hirschmüller, *Life and Work of Josef Breuer,* 95–132 and 276–308.

45   *the unique harmony:* Ibid., 121.

46   *Forgive me, I am:* Ibid., 121.

46   *Love did not come to me:* Ibid., 308.

CHAPTER FIVE: MEANING OUT OF CHAOS

Unless otherwise indicated, all quotations dealing with the cases are taken from *Studies on Hysteria.* Information about Anna von Lieben is found in Swales, "Freud, His Teacher, and the Birth of Psychoanalysis" and about Aurelia Kronich in Swales, "Freud, Katharina, and the First 'Wild Analysis'." Information on these and other of Freud's cases can also be found in Appignanesi and Forrester, *Freud's Women.*

49   *really the Baroness Anna von Lieben:* Additional information about von Lieben can be found in Freud (with Breuer), *Studies,* 69–70 and 176–181.

50   *The only way:* Ibid., 70.

51   *Suddenly, she put:* Ibid., 178.

51   *I have not:* Ibid., 180.

52   *Baroness Fanny Moser:* For an interesting discussion of "Emmy von N.," see Bromberg, "Hysteria, Dissociation, and Cure."

52   *unusual degree of:* Freud (with Breuer), *Studies,* 48–49.

53   *She was probably:* Ibid., 49.

53   *When I was five:* Ibid., 52, 55.

53   *morally over-sensitive personality:* Ibid., 65.

53   *She was brought:* Ibid., 49.

54   *The baby had been:* Ibid., 60.

54   *His relatives, who:* Ibid., 63.

54   *My therapy consists:* Ibid., 53.

55   *said in a definitely:* Ibid., 63.

55   *She described her:* Ibid., 63.

55   *pathogenic reminiscences of:* Ibid., 56.

55   *Specific phobias were:* Ibid., 87 and 89.

56   *amongst all the intimate:* Ibid., 103.

56   *It is necessary:* Ibid., 88.

57   *She had not married:* Ibid., 103. Women in nineteenth-century Austria-Hungary had few property rights. If she had married again, her new husband would have controlled all her wealth, thus depriving her and her daughters of any control of the money.

57   *her "erotic extravagance":* Appignanesi and Forrester, *Freud's Women*, 98.

57   *My patient's condition:* Freud (with Breuer), *Studies*, 77.

57   *by an act of will:* Ibid., 77 and 78.

58   *storms in her head:* Ibid., 78.

58   *which lasted eight weeks:* See Strachey in ibid., 307.

58   *I think they come:* Ibid., 82.

58   *fought against the:* Ibid., 101.

58   *The therapeutic success:* Ibid., 101.

59   *"morally serious," respectable:* Ibid., 103.

60   *a salon hostess:* Appignanesi and Forrester, *Freud's Women*, 92.

61   *I decided to start:* Ibid., 110.

61   *joined in a little:* Ibid., 115.

62   *I believe that:* Ibid., 117.

62   *An idea must be:* Ibid., 123.

63   *someone's standing behind:* Ibid., 126.

63   *you must have seen:* Ibid., 127.

64   *there was a hammering:* Ibid., 128.

64   *gave way to a:* Ibid., 132.

64   *a mere suspicion of:* Ibid., 134.

65   *the first full-length analysis:* Ibid., 138 and 139.

65   *This procedure was:* Ibid., 139.

65   *he did not fail:* Ibid., 140.

66   *the independence of her:* Ibid., 161.

66   *In all these:* Ibid., 135.

66   *acutely her helplessness:* Ibid., 141 and 143–144.

67   *reproached herself most:* Ibid., 146.

67 *encouraged her to:* Ibid., 149.

67 *discussed every kind:* Ibid., 155.

67 *now forced itself:* Ibid., 156 and 157.

67 *This girl felt:* Ibid., 157.

68 *friendly interest in her:* Ibid., 158.

68 *married someone unknown:* Ibid., 160.

68 *just a young:* Quoted in Gay, *Freud*, 72 and 665.

68 *the "interest shown:* Freud (with Breuer), *Studies*, 138 and 158.

CHAPTER SIX: AMONG THE AFFLICTED

71 *differences were mounting:* The fact that Breuer did not feel that their views were shared is brought out in letters they exchanged between 1907 and 1908 about the publication of a new edition of *Studies*; these letters were recently made available to me by Jim Lieberman.

72 *no suspicion of:* Freud (with Breuer), *Studies*, 3.

72 *As a rule it is:* Ibid., 3.

73 *Each individual hysterical:* Ibid., 6.

73 *An injury that:* Ibid., 8.

74 *It may therefore:* Ibid., 11.

74 *A neuralgia may follow:* Ibid., 5.

74 *It has cost enough:* Freud to Fliess, Masson, *Complete Letters*, 36–37.

75 *I willingly adhere:* Freud (with Breuer), *Studies*, 286.

76 *that the great majority:* Ibid., 246.

76 *of a refined organization:* Ibid., 245.

76 *In contrasting the hypnoid:* Breuer's discussion of defense and hypnoid states is in ibid., 214–215.

76 *not because one:* Ibid., 214.

77 *Alongside sexual hysteria:* Ibid., 247.

77 *One point on which:* Breuer in Masson, *Complete Letters*, 151.

77 *I think of the underhandedness:* Freud to Fliess, Masson, *Complete Letters*, 304–305.

77 *The attempt that has:* Freud (with Breuer), *Studies*, 250.

78 Freud's discussion of defense is found in ibid., 257–260.

78 *Were you ashamed:* Ibid., 117.

79 *boy had run off in fear:* Ibid., 211–212.

79 *a number of more:* Ibid., 213.

79 *abused him in the:* Ibid., 14.

79 *Fraulein Rosalia H.:* Ibid., 169–173.

80   *a gifted lady:* Ibid., 162–163.

80   *when her dog died:* Ibid., 273.

80   *a stuporous condition:* Ibid., 275.

80   *lady who had suffered:* Ibid., 276.

81   *It still strikes me:* Ibid., 160.

81   *was often in tears:* Ibid., 78.

CHAPTER SEVEN: FREUD'S "ONLY OTHER"

83   *Both authors have:* Quoted in Ellenberger, *Discovery of the Unconscious,* 772.

84   *saw Freud approaching:* Hanna Breuer (Breuer's daughter-in-law) to Ernest Jones, April 21, 1954, quoted in Roazen, *Freud,* 80, 558, 2417. For further examples of Freud's hostility to Breuer, see Freud to Fliess, Masson, *Complete Letters,* 170 and 175.

86   *Emma Eckstein:* The full details of the Eckstein episode are covered in Breger, *Freud,* 131–133 and 402.

86   *mystical nonsense:* Freud to Fliess, Masson, *Complete Letters,* 310.

87   *I hope the path:* Ibid., 356.

87   *Esteemed friend and:* Ibid., 15.

88   *Your kind should not:* Ibid., 158.

88   *We are now living:* Ibid., 54.

89   *The children and wife:* Ibid., 68.

CHAPTER EIGHT: INVENTING A UNIVERSAL "SCIENTIFIC" LAW

92   *It may be taken:* Freud's speculations on the role of sexuality in a variety of neurotic conditions can be found in the Fliess letters, Masson, *Complete Letters,* 39–147, and elsewhere.

92   *society appears doomed:* Masson, *Complete Letters,* 44.

92   *The idea that women:* Ideas about the relationship of "hysteria" to woman's sexual "discharge" are discussed in detail in Maines, *Technology of Orgasm.*

92   *By the time he:* Freud to Fliess, Masson, *Complete Letters,* 202.

93   *the most important:* Freud, *Interpretation of Dreams,* 317.

93   *Perhaps most troubling:* The importance of the loss of Breuer was first pointed out by Otto Rank; see Lieberman, *Acts of Will,* 323.

93   *told me a great deal:* Freud to Fliess, Masson, *Complete Letters,* 268.

93   *I shall be grateful:* Ibid., 269.

94   *between two and two:* Ibid., 268.

94   *The expectation of:* Ibid., 266.

95   *I no longer believe* and following quotations: Ibid., 264–265.

95   *A single idea of:* Ibid., 272.

95   *Freud's substitution of his:* The contrast between his father and Oedipus—a play Freud knew well because he was required to translate it from the Greek for his final examination in the Gymnasium—is most instructive. Freud had recalled the memory from his boyhood of his father passively complying when told "Jew, get off the sidewalk," which Sigmund tied to his identification with the warrior Hannibal. In Sophocles's play, the young Oedipus encounters Laius, king of Thebes—who turns out to be Oedipus's own father—and is ordered off the road and struck by a staff. Far from complying, he grabs the weapon and beats Laius and other members of the royal party to death.

97   *If hysterical subjects:* Freud, *On the History,* 17–18.

98   *a "conquistador" as he later:* Zantop, in *Colonial Fantasies,* points out that textbooks used in schools such as those Freud attended as a boy glorified the exploits of Cortez.

CHAPTER NINE: FULL CIRCLE

100 *So many excellent:* Freud (with Breuer), *Studies,* 250.

100 *as "Dora" she became:* There is a large secondary literature on the Dora case. The best overall discussion can be found in Patrick Mahony's insightful *Freud's Dora,* which contains references to many other works. See also Bernheimer and Kahane, *In Dora's Case;* and Decker, *Freud, Dora, Vienna.*

101 *were all in place by 1905:* Two significant exceptions are the discussion of trauma, mastery, and turning passive into active in the opening chapters of *Beyond the Pleasure Principle* and the reformulation of the theory of anxiety in *Inhibitions, Symptoms, and Anxiety.*

102 *the historian Paul Roazen:* See Roazen, *How Freud Worked.*

102 *When Freud wrote about:* For an account of the way case histories were presented in the years before Freud, see Frust, *Before Freud.* Pierre Janet was the only medical authority who wrote about his patients as people rather than as specimens.

103 *a perfect presentation:* Kardiner, *My Analysis with Freud,* 37.

103 *The first mask you:* Ibid., 61.

103 *on a wild-goose chase:* Ibid., 98.

103   *his unruly homosexual libido:* Jones, *Life and Work*, 317.

104   *I cannot put up:* Freud, *On Beginning the Treatment*, 134.

105   *When Freud followed:* For a comprehensive account of how Freud actu-
       ally worked with his patients, see Lynn and Vaillant, "Anonymity,
       Neutrality, and Confidentiality."

106   *Symbols allow us in:* Freud, *Interpretation of Dreams*, 151.

106   *Three Essays on the Theory:* Although those who accept Freud's myth
       about his originality credit him as the one who more or less invented
       "infantile sexuality," more recent research has shown that a number
       of other investigators, called "sexologists," were working in this area,
       some of them before Freud. See Sulloway, *Freud, Biologist of the Mind*,
       for a comprehensive discussion.

106   *about masturbation:* Freud's own views about masturbation were mixed,
       though in general his effect was to depathologize the practice. See
       Breger, *Freud*, 185–187.

107   *It often happens:* Freud, *Three Essays on the Theory of Sexuality*, 228.

109   *It has justly been:* Ibid., 226. Note Freud's rhetorical style here, which
       carries the argument more than evidence, or even examples. "It has
       justly been said" by whom? The use of the passive voice throughout
       makes it seem as if everyone accepts these ideas rather than present-
       ing them as Freud's own doctrines. "Every new arrival on this planet"
       is certainly a forceful assertion—yet again, where is the evidence?
       Much anthropological work had been done by 1920, though Freud, as
       was typical, confined himself to "psychoanalytic studies," that is, the
       work of disciples who agreed with his doctrines lest they be branded
       dissidents and expelled from the movement.

111   *much more straightforward:* See Freud's comment, made in *Studies* before
       he invented his complex Oedipal theory of conscience formation,
       that Fanny Moser's tendency to "self-depreciation" is related to her
       upbringing by an "overly energetic and severe" mother.

111   *It is one of the tragedies:* The most detailed discussion of the "resolution
       of the Oedipus complex" can be found in Freud, *Ego and the Id*. Freud
       had a deep belief in Oedipal motives, thinking that every one of his
       followers, many of whom revered him as the father they never had, at
       the deepest level wanted to kill him and take his place. It was this
       same belief that led him to prohibit his three sons from entering his
       own field, medicine.

112   *It was anxiety which* and the following quotations: Freud, *Inhibitions,
       Symptoms, and Anxiety*, 32.

113   *The last and decisive:* Graf, "Reminiscences," 471.

113 *"The Committee," whose:* See Grosskurth, *Secret Ring,* for a complete account of the formation and functioning of this group.

115 *It is, however, a significant:* Freud, *"Introduction" to Psycho-Analysis and the War Neuroses,* 207. Not only was he oblivious to the shell-shocked veterans in Vienna, he does not appear to have talked with his three sons about their war experiences, even though all of them had served in the Austrian Army.

116 *sex researcher Havelock Ellis:* For a full account of changes in views of women, see Russell, *Sexual Science.*

BIBLIOGRAPHY

Appignanesi, Lisa, and John Forrester. *Freud's Women*. London: Virago Press, 1992.

Atwood, George E., and Robert D. Stolorow. "Freud." In *Faces in a Cloud: Subjectivity in Personality Theory*. 2nd ed. New York: Jason Aronson, 1993.

Bernays, Anna. "My Brother Sigmund Freud." *American Mercury* LI (1940): 336.

Bernheimer, Charles, and Claire Kahane, eds. *In Dora's Case: Freud-Hysteria-Feminism*. New York: Columbia University Press, 1985.

Blanton, Smiley. *Diary of My Analysis with Sigmund Freud*. New York: Hawthorn Books, 1971.

Borch-Jacobson, Mikkel. *Remembering Anna O.: A Century of Mystification*. Trans. Kirby Olson. New York: Routledge, 1996.

Bowlby, John. *Attachment and Loss. Volume 1: Attachment*. New York: Basic Books, 1969.

———. *Attachment and Loss. Volume 2: Separation*. New York: Basic Books, 1973.

Breger, Louis. *Freud: Darkness in the Midst of Vision*. New York: John Wiley & Sons, 2000.

Boehlich, Walter, ed. *The Letters of Sigmund Freud to Eduard Silberstein: 1871–1881*. Translated by Arnold J. Pomerans. Cambridge, MA: Harvard University Press, 1990.

Bromberg, Philip M. "Hysteria, Dissociation, and Cure: Emmy von N. Revisited." *Psychoanalytic Dialogues* 6 (1996): 55–71.

———. *Standing in the Spaces: Essays on Clinical Process, Trauma and Dissociation*. Hillsdale, N.J.: Analytic Press, 1998.

Byck, Robert, ed. *Cocaine Papers by Sigmund Freud*. New York: New American Library, 1974.

Clark, Ronald W. *Freud: The Man and the Cause*. New York: Random House, 1980.

Cranefield, Paul F. "Josef Breuer's Evaluation of His Contribution to Psychoanalysis." *International Journal of Psycho-Analysis* 39 (1958): 319–322.

Decker, Hannah S. *Freud, Dora, Vienna, 1900*. New York: Free Press, 1991.

Dorsey, John M. *An American Psychiatrist in Vienna, 1935–1937, and His Sigmund Freud*. Detroit: Center for Health Education, 1976.

Ellenberger, Henri F. *The Discovery of the Unconscious: The History and Evolution of Dynamic Psychiatry.* New York: Basic Books, 1970.

———. "The Story of Anna O.: A Critical Review of New Data." *Journal of the History of the Behavioral Sciences* 8 (1972): 267–279.

Engelman, Edmund. *Bergasse 19: Sigmund Freud's Home and Offices, Vienna 1938.* Chicago: University of Chicago Press, 1976.

Ferenczi, Sandor. *The Clinical Diary of Sandor Ferenczi.* Ed. Judith Dupont. Trans. Michael Balint and Nicola Z. Jackson. Cambridge, MA: Harvard University Press, 1995.

Freeman, Lucy. *The Story of Anna O.* New York: Walker, 1972.

Freud, Ernst L., ed. *The Letters of Sigmund Freud.* Translated by Tania Stern and James Stern. New York: Basic Books, 1960.

Freud, Martin. *Sigmund Freud: Man and Father.* New York: Vanguard Press, 1958.

Freud, Sigmund. *On Aphasia: A Critical Study* [1891]. New York: International University Press, 1953.

The following titles by Freud are from *The Standard Edition of the Complete Psychological Works of Sigmund Freud,* edited and translated by James Strachey, in collaboration with Anna Freud, assisted by Alix Strachey and Alan Tyson. London: Hogarth Press. Works are cited by title, volume, date, and page number.

Freud, Sigmund (with Josef Breuer). *Studies on Hysteria* 2 (1895): 1–309.

Freud, Sigmund. *The Aetiology of Hysteria* 3 (1896): 189–221.

———. *Sexuality in the Aetiology of the Neuroses* 3 (1898): 261–285.

———. *The Interpretation of Dreams* 4 and 5 (1900): 1–627.

———. *The Psychopathology of Everyday Life* 6 (1901): 1–310.

———. *Fragment of an Analysis of a Case of Hysteria* 7 (1905): 3–122.

———. *Three Essays on the Theory of Sexuality* 7 (1905): 125–243.

———. *"Civilized" Sexual Morality and Modern Nervous Illness* 9 (1908): 177–204.

———. *Analysis of a Phobia in a Five-Year-Old Boy* 10 (1909): 3–149.

———. *Notes Upon a Case of Obsessional Neurosis* 10 (1909): 153–326.

———. *Five Lectures on Psychoanalysis* 11 (1910): 3–36.

———. *The Handling of Dream-Interpretation in Psychoanalysis* 12 (1911): 85–96.

———. *Psychoanalytic Notes on an Autobiographical Account of a Case of Paranoia (Dementia Paranoids)* 12 (1911): 3–82.

———. *The Dynamics of the Transference* 12 (1912): 97–108.

———. *Recommendations to Physicians Practicing Psycho-Analysis* 12 (1912): 109–120.

———. *Totem and Taboo* 13 (1912): 1–161.

———. *On Beginning the Treatment (Further Recommendations on the Technique of Psycho-Analysis, I)* 12 (1913): 121–144.

———. *Observations on Transference-Love (Further Recommendations on the Technique of Psycho-Analysis III)* 12 (1914): 157–171.

———. *On the History of the Psycho-Analytic Movement* 14 (1914): 3–66.

———. *Remembering, Repeating and Working-Through (Further Recommendations on the Technique of Psychoanalysis II)* 12 (1914): 145–156.

———. *Some Reflections on Schoolboy Psychology* 13 (1914): 241–244.

———. *Some Character Types Met with in Psychoanalytic Work* 14 (1916): 309–333.

———. *From the History of an Infantile Neurosis* 17 (1918): 3–122.

———. *"Introduction" to Psycho-Analysis and the War Neuroses* 17 (1919): 206–210.

———. *Beyond the Pleasure Principle* 18 (1920): 3–64.

———. *The Psychogenesis of a Case of Homosexuality in a Woman* 18 (1920): 145–172.

———. *The Ego and the Id* 19 (1923): 3–66.

———. *An Autobiographical Study* 20 (1925): 77–174.

———. *Inhibitions, Symptoms, and Anxiety* 20 (1926): 77–174.

———. *Female Sexuality* 21 (1931): 223–243.

———. *New Introductory Lectures on Psycho-Analysis* 22 (1933): 3–182.

———. *Analysis Terminable and Interminable* 23 (1937): 211–253.

———. *Moses and Monotheism: Three Essays* 23 (1939): 3–137.

Fromm, Erich. *Sigmund Freud's Mission: An Analysis of His Personality and Influence.* New York: Grove Press, 1959.

Frust, Lillian R. *Before Freud: Hysteria and Hypnosis in Later Nineteenth-Century Psychiatric Cases.* Lewisburg, Pa.: Bucknell University Press, 2008.

Gay, Peter. *Freud: A Life for Our Time.* New York: W. W. Norton, 1988.

Graf, Max. "Reminiscences of Professor Sigmund Freud." *Psychoanalytic Quarterly* 11 (1942): 465–476.

Grosskurth, Phyllis. *The Secret Ring: Freud's Inner Circle and the Politics of Psychoanalysis.* Reading, Mass.: Addison-Wesley, 1991.

Guillain, Georges. *J. M. Charcot, His Life, His Work.* London: Pitman Medical Publishing, 1959.

H. D. [Hilda Doolittle]. *Tribute to Freud.* New York: New Directions, 1956.

Heller, Judith Berneys. "Freud's Mother and Father." In *Freud as We Knew Him,* edited by Hendrik M. Ruitenbeek, 334–340. Detroit: Wayne State University Press, 1973.

Hirschmüller, Albrecht. *The Life and Work of Josef Breuer: Physiology and Psychoanalysis.* New York: New York University Press, 1989.

Jones, Ernest. *The Life and Work of Sigmund Freud.* Volume 1: *The Formative Years and the Great Discoveries, 1856–1900.* New York: Basic Books, 1953.

Kardiner, Abram, *My Analysis with Freud: Reminiscences.* New York: W. W. Norton, 1977.

Laforgue, Rene. "Personal Memories of Freud." In *Freud as We Knew Him,* edited by Hendrik M. Ruitenbeek, 341–349. Detroit: Wayne State University Press, 1973.

Lieberman, E. James. *Acts of Will: The Life and Work of Otto Rank*. New York: Free Press, 1985.

Lynn, David J., and George E. Vaillant. "Anonymity, Neutrality, and Confidentiality in the Actual Methods of Sigmund Freud: A Review of Forty-Three Cases, 1907–1939." *American Journal of Psychiatry* 155, no. 2 (1998): 163–171.

Mahony, Patrick J. *Freud's Dora: A Psychoanalytic, Historical and Textual Study*. New Haven, CT: Yale University Press, 1996.

Main, Mary, N. Kaplan, and J. Cassidy. "Security in Infancy, Childhood and Adulthood: A Move to the Level of Representation." *Monographs of the Society for Research in Child Development* 50, nos. 1–2, Serial No. 209 (1985): 66–104.

Maines, Rachel P. *The Technology of Orgasm: "Hysteria," the Vibrator, and Woman's Sexual Satisfaction*. Baltimore, MD: Johns Hopkins University Press, 1999.

Masson, Jeffrey M., ed. and trans. *The Complete Letters of Sigmund Freud to Wilhelm Fliess: 1887–1904*. Cambridge, MA: Harvard University Press, 1985.

McGuire, William, ed. *The Freud/Jung Letters: The Correspondence between Sigmund Freud and C. G. Jung*. Translated by Ralph Manheim and R. F. C. Hull. Princeton, NJ: Princeton University Press, 1974.

Mitchell, Steven A. *Relational Concepts in Psychoanalysis*. Cambridge, MA: Harvard University Press, 1988.

Pappenheim, Bertha [Anna O.]. *In the Junk Shop and Other Stories*. Translated by Renate Latimer. Riverside, Calif.: Ariadne Press, 2008.

Rank, Otto. *The Trauma of Birth* [1924]. New York: Robert Brunner, 1952.

Roazen, Paul. *Freud and His Followers*. New York: Knopf, 1975.

———. *How Freud Worked: First-Hand Accounts of Patients*. Northvale, NJ: Jason Aronson, 1995.

Rosenbaum, Max, and Melvin Muroff, eds. *Anna O.: Fourteen Contemporary Perspectives*. New York: Free Press, 1984.

Ruitenbeek, Hendrik M., ed. *Freud as We Knew Him*. Detroit: Wayne State University Press, 1973.

Russett, Cynthia E. *Sexual Science: The Victorian Construction of Womanhood*. Cambridge, MA: Harvard University Press, 1989.

Schnitzler, Arthur. *My Youth in Vienna*. Translated by Catherine Hutter. New York: Holt, Rinehart & Winston, 1970.

Sprengnether, Madelon. "Enforcing Oedipus: Freud and Dora." In *In Dora's Case: Freud-Hysteria-Feminism*, edited by Charles Bernheimer and Claire Kahane, 254–276. New York: Columbia University Press, 1985.

Stolorow, Robert D., Bernard Brandschaft, and George E. Atwood. *Psychoanalytic Treatment: An Intersubjective Approach*. Hillsdale, NJ: Analytic Press, 1987.

Sulloway, Frank J. *Freud, Biologist of the Mind: Beyond the Psychoanalytic Legend*. New York: Basic Books, 1979.

Swales, Peter J. "Freud, His Teacher, and the Birth of Psychoanalysis." In *Freud: Appraisals and Reappraisals: Contributions to Freud Studies,* edited by Paul E. Stepansky, Vol. 1, 3–82. Hillsdale, NJ: Analytic Press, 1986.

————. "Freud, Katharina, and the First 'Wild Analysis'." In *Freud: Appraisals and Reappraisals: Contributions to Freud Studies,* edited by Paul E. Stepansky, Vol. 3, 79–164. Hillsdale, NJ: Analytic Press, 1988.

————. "Freud, Minna Bernays, and the Conquest of Rome: New Light on the Origins of Psychoanalysis." *New American Review* 1 (1982): 1–23.

Swenson, Carol R. "Freud's 'Anna O.': Social Work's Bertha Pappenheim." *Clinical Social Work Journal* 22 (1994): 149–163.

Veith, Ilza. *Hysteria: The History of a Disease.* Chicago: University of Chicago Press, 1965.

Wallin, David J. *Attachment in Psychotherapy.* New York: Guildford Press, 2007.

Wolff, Larry. *Postcards from the End of the World: Child Abuse in Freud's Vienna.* New York: Athenaeum, 1988.

Wortis, Joseph. *Fragments of an Analysis with Freud.* New York: Simon & Schuster, 1954.

Zantop, Susanne. *Colonial Fantasies: Conquest, Family, and Nation in Precolonial Germany, 1770–1870.* Durham, NC: Duke University Press, 1997.

INDEX

Basic Ideas

Every great idea—whether embodied in a speech, a mathematical equation, a song, or a work of art—has an origin, a birth, and a life of enduring influence. In each book in the Basic Ideas series, a leading authority offers a concise biography of a text that transformed its world, and ours.